$20.00

COWBOYS
IN UNIFORM

COVER: "THRE'LL BE A HOT TIME IN THE OLD TOWN TONIGHT, MY BABY." 24 1/4 x 19 3/16 oil on canvas by Frederic Remington circa 1898. Courtesy the Art Institute of Chicago, copyright 1998. Coining a title from a popular song of the period "A Hot Time In The Old Town Tonight" became the Rough Rider regimental song. The subject in the painting is in proper Rough Rider uniform, although the hat appears to be non-regulation.

Photograph of Troop K taken in Tampa, Florida, perhaps just prior to leaving for Port Tampa. Cartridge belts appear to be full. The trooper reclining right of center holding carbine in left hand is wearing an empty holster. The trooper standing near the tent is wearing light-colored trousers of unknown origin. An officer is seen standing just right of center, possibly Lt. Carr. Image courtesy of PPLM.

IN UNIFORM

By
J.C. Stewart

Dedicated to the memory of
Frank M. Tejeda of
San Antonio, Texas
Oct. 2, 1945 - Jan. 30, 1997

Copyright 1998
Rough Rider Publishing Co.
1095 Aspen Way
Show Low, AZ 85901

All rights reserved. No part of this publication may be reproduced, stored in a retrieval system or transmitted in any form or by any means, electronic or mechanical or otherwise without the written permission of the publisher.

ISBN 0-9662682-0-2

Library of Congress 98-065694

Written by J.C. Stewart
Photographs by David L. Widmaier
Cover design by George Pinter
Edited by Joan Baeza

All photographs used with permission of the owners.

ABBREVIATIONS

SHM	Sharlot Hall Museum, Prescott, Arizona
RRM	Rough Rider Museum, Las Vegas, N.M.
AHS	Arizona Historical Society, Tucson, Arizona
HHLRC	Harvard Houghton Library, Roosevelt Collection Cambridge, Massachusetts
FSH	Fort Sam Houston Museum, San Antonio, Texas
PPLM	Phoenix Public Library McClintock Collection
DWP	David L. Widmaier Photograph
DBP	Don Beardsley Photograph
NTP	Norm Tessman Photograph
MNM	Museum of New Mexico, Santa Fe, New Mexico
OHS	Oklahoma Historical Society

Contents

Preface	1
Introduction	2
Enlisted Men's Uniforms	4
Khaki, The Second Uniform	9
McCurdy Letters	11
Allen McCurdy's Diary	15
Officers' Uniforms	18
Accouterments	23
Color Plates	28
Weapons	45
Horses, Horse Equipments and Dismounted Pack	54
Dismounted Pack and Shelter	60
Regimental Flags	64
Personal Items and Mementos	69
Summary	72
Excerpts from 1896 Cavalry Drill Manual	73

Preface

My interest in the 1st U.S. Volunteer Cavalry, Rough Riders began in 1980 while employed as an aide at the Sharlot Hall Museum, Prescott, Arizona. Already an avid student of U.S. military history, I was naturally drawn to the original Rough Rider artifacts and pictures found in the museum collection. The following 18 years found me constantly "on the prowl" for any information pertaining to the Rough Riders story or their issued uniforms or equipment. The information in this text is the result of that research to date. Surviving identified artifacts from the Sharlot Hall Museum, Arizona Historical Society, the Rough Rider Museum, Ft. Sam Houston, and items from the personal collections of Hayes Otoupalik and the authors are disclosed. Careful examination of identified Rough Rider photographs from the Phoenix and Harvard Library Collections are discussed herein.

Valid attempts to secure official reports or data from government sources pertaining to Rough Riders met with little success. The Department of the Army's Center of Military History, the Division of Armed Forces History National Museum, Smithsonian Institution and the National Archives Military Reference Branch all had limited or no information on the First U.S. Volunteer Cavalry issue. One source of potential information I was unable to access was a collection of letters and notes compiled by surviving Rough Riders, kept at the Harvard College Houghton Library. The quest for Rough Rider information is not over.

I cannot take sole credit for this project and feel compelled to acknowledge the following people for their assistance: Michael Carmen, Brad Dahlquist, Wallace Daily, Witt Edwards, Fay Freed, Charles Herner, Adrianne Jeske, Burbank Jung, Dave Jones, David Key, Melanie LaBorwit, Mike Lewis, Mindi Love, John Manguso, Hayes Otoupalik, Tom Peterson, Mark Santiago, Robert Serio, Kathleen Sheedy, Norm Tessman, Jay VanOrdan, Kimberly Wageman, and Michael Woodcock.

Special thanks go to my publishing partner, David L. Widmaier, for his photographic talents and patience.

Warmest appreciation must go to the fine gentlemen that modeled the uniforms in this book: Christopher DeMille, Casey Murph, and Robert Overacker.

I've saved the best for last, my top notch support team, Cheryl, Corinna and Rachel.

J.C. Stewart
1998

Introduction

The story of the 1st U.S. Volunteer Cavalry of 1898 has become American military legend. Though it is a century later, most every adult in this country has heard or knows something about this famous regiment known simply as the Rough Riders. They enjoyed a swell of popularity during their own time as well. A mere mention of the Rough Riders in 1898 brought a sense of excitement to all but the most sedate. Every young man wanted to be one, young ladies wanted the buttons of their uniforms, and school boys at play pretended they were Roosevelt leading the Rough Riders in a gallant charge. Returning soldiers of other U.S. regiments found themselves being asked on the street by patriotic citizens if they were a part of the brave Rough Riders. It is likely a few of these confronted soldiers pondered this question carefully as a free drink at the local beer garden might just ride on the answer. People loved them and all wanted to know what these fighting men from the nation's last wild territories looked like. Journalists and photographers were quick to respond to the public need. A media blitz followed the Rough Riders everywhere and they discovered their willing subjects weren't camera shy.

The number of photographs taken of this unit is impressive. A hundred years later, we can still see them being recruited, in transport, being trained in combat, convalescing, and attending reunions. You name it, there is probably a picture of a Rough Rider doing it.

Close examination of some so-called Rough Rider photographs reveal puzzling discrepancies. When these pictures are compared with solid historical research and attributed archival material many mistakes or flaws start turning up in the time, place, or subject matter of the photo in question. For instance, a photo of Roosevelt taken in September of '98 at Camp Wikoff is labeled as San Antonio May '98, or even worse, a picture of regular infantry crossing a river in Cuba is wrongly identified as being Rough Riders.

Some of the written information about the uniforms and equipment of Rough Riders is also misleading. Oddly enough, some of this confusion comes from the Rough Riders themselves, in the way of reminiscing or interviews done later in life about their experiences.

Sadly these mistakes remain to this day and are found uncorrected in accepted reference books currently available to the Rough Rider student.

A recently released movie (summer 1997) about the Rough Riders, while a sincere effort, and entertaining, stubbornly ignored the truth and "Hollywoodized" the Rough Rider image. Once again historical accuracy was sacrificed to sell a movie.

This misinformation and legend status creates a kind of mythology about the subject which in time, left unchanged, becomes accepted fact. This fact versus myth dilemma produces an odd paradox among students of history. To quote a friend, Mike Lewis, "I've seen many examples of sincere people doing research to support a preconception they gained long ago and doggedly ignoring facts in the process." To further confuse our subject, enlisted men of the 1st Volunteer Cavalry, 1898, received two distinct issues of uniforms during their short time in service. The many photographs taken of the Rough Riders at Camp Wikoff show them in a hodge-podge mixture of both the m-1884 and the m-1898 uniform worn at the personal whim of the individual, while a few others, mostly late-comers to the regiment, actually had to purchase their own uniforms from military clothiers in San Antonio prior to enlisting.

The enormous advantage the 1st U.S. Volunteer Cavalry had in leadership over other newly raised regiments struggling to acquire uniforms and equipments can't be overestimated. Following the declaration of war with Spain, the standing regular army of just over 28,000 officers and enlisted men were quickly augmented with two calls from President McKinley for another 200,000 volunteers. Stockpiles of items essential to these new volunteers would soon be exhausted. Those regimental commanders wishing to see their men equipped had to move quickly and be first in line at the quartermaster. It also helped to exercise any and all influence one might have.

The following lines are from Theodore Roosevelt's book *The Rough Riders*. His own words best sum up the advantage they possessed.

"There was one topic to which, in our talking (Wood and Roosevelt) we returned, and that was that

2

possible war with Spain. We both felt very strongly that such a war would be as righteous as it would be advantageous to the honor and the interests of the nation...We then at once began to try to see we had our share of it. The President and my own chief, Secretary Long...would help me. Wood was the medical advisor of both the President and the Secretary of War, and could count upon their friendship. So we started with the odds in our favor.

"Wood and I were speedily commissioned as Colonel and Lieutenant-Colonel of the First United States Volunteer Cavalry.

"The difficulty lay in arming, equipping, mounting and disciplining the men we selected. Hundreds of regiments were being called into existence by the national government, and each regiment was sure to have innumerable wants to be satisfied. To a man who knew the ground as Wood did, and who was entirely aware of our national unpreparedness, it was evident that the ordnance and quartermaster's bureaus could not meet, for some time to come, one-tenth of the demands that would be made upon them; and it was all-important to get in first with our demands. Thanks to his knowledge of the situation and promptness, we immediately put in our requisitions for the articles indispensable for the equipment of the regiment; and by the ceaseless worrying of excellent bureaucrats, who had no idea how to do things quickly or how to meet an emergency, we succeeded in getting our rifles, cartridges, revolvers, clothing, shelter-tents, and horse gear just in time to enable us to go on with the Santiago expedition. Some of the State troops, who were already organized as National Guards, were, of course, ready, after a fashion, when the war broke out, but no other regiment which had our work to do was able to do it in anything like as quick time, and therefore no other volunteer regiment saw anything like the fighting which we did."

It is my contention that good photographic evidence remains the best source of reliable information on the Rough Riders' uniforms and equipment.

Close examination can reveal the exact type and model of objects found in the image or start a new course of research to determine the identity of an unknown piece seen in the photograph.

Work on this book began in November 1996. Seen here for the first time are original surviving Rough Rider uniforms and artifacts, and rarely viewed photographs of the men with their issued gear.

With the printing of this book, I hope to aid the Rough Rider student in his search for the truth, and in a small way to help uphold the honor of these brave volunteers of 1898.

J.C. Stewart
1998

Half of original stereo view card, H Troop. Author's collection.

Enlisted Men's Uniforms

The uniform issued to the men arriving at their training facility outside San Antonio, Texas, might not have been what they were expecting. Handed them by the quartermaster was a brown canvas uniform, not the traditional dark blue wool coat and mid-blue pants worn throughout the rest of the army.

The distinctive brown canvas dress of the Rough Riders was in fact an official uniform of the regular U.S. Army. The Model 1884 fatigue uniform was issued to most enlisted men in service at that time. Adopted on May 31, 1884, the brown fatigue uniform was intended for "each enlisted man of the Army who may be required to work on extra daily, or fatigue duty." [1] It seems the only purpose of the 1884 fatigues was to save the finer, more expensive wool service uniform from harsh wear while manual labor was being performed.[2] Quartermaster specifications for the canvas sack coat and trousers were: the coat, "to be a single-breasted sack coat, with falling collar and having six India rubber buttons in front from waist to neck, to have an outside pocket sewn on each breast." The canvas trousers are "to have slanting top pockets, a watch pocket and a hip pocket on the right side, straps and buckles; waist-band and flies faced with the same material the trousers are made of." [3] Both coat and trousers were made of six-ounce cotton duck dyed brown, and came in a range of six sizes, a No. 1 being the smallest.

During the three decades prior to the war with Spain, fatigues or canvas clothing of some variation had been issued from time to time by the army. Although made out of wool, the standard four-button jacket or blouse used by federal troops during the Civil War 33 years earlier was in fact a fatigue coat that became the accepted uniform of the period. At times the army had provided lightweight summer clothing for its men. By the late 1880s, an unbleached cotton duck uniform was authorized for troops stationed in "extreme southern latitudes," but saw limited use.[4] Simple canvas stable frocks also were issued to mounted soldiers during this period.

It seems evident that procurement of the Model 1884 fatigue uniform for the Rough Riders was a conscious effort on the part of Colonel Leonard Wood, and not just the luck of the draw from the quartermaster. In the summer of 1886, Wood had served with the 4th United States Cavalry as it pursued Geronimo and his band of Apaches over some of the worst-imaginable terrain in Arizona and Northern Mexico. There's little doubt he learned firsthand the limitations of the wool service uniform during that campaign. Colonel Wood wanted the best for his troops, and the Rough Riders got the practical fatigues as their service uniform.[5] *Please refer to figures 4, 5, 6 and 7 of the color plates.*

Worn under the sack coat, but used primarily as an outer garment during much of the Cuba campaign, is the model 1883 overshirt.

A dark blue wool flannel pullover shirt was adopted November 26, 1883. This loose fitting shirt featured a falling collar, three hard rubber buttons on a 2-inch front plait, two outside "patch" breast pockets about 7 inches deep by 6 inches wide, rounded at the bottoms, with button closure, complete with round-off buttoned cuffs.[6]

A dark blue wool shirt has few redeeming qualities to the wearer during a mid-summer campaign in the tropics.[7] However, it is unlikely the soldier could be mistaken as an enemy while wearing Union blue by an inexperienced invading U.S. Army. Though admittedly hot, period photographs of the army well into the campaign revealed few soldiers "lost" their shirts or even took them off.

A Model 1883 overshirt, with Rough Rider provenience, fortunately still exists, once the issue shirt of A Troop Pvt, Arthur L. Tuttle of Safford, Arizona Territory. This rare shirt was presented to Charles Herner of Tucson, Arizona, author of the *Arizona Rough Riders*. The shirt was given to Herner by Tuttle during a series of interviews in the mid 1960s.

The Tuttle shirt is a textbook example of the Model 1883 overshirt. It is in relatively good condition, though heavily worn with the elbows entirely worn through. Attached to the upper left shoulder is a hand-written note from Tuttle's mother stating, "Archie Tuttle's shirt that he fought in before Santiago, Cuba."

To the author's knowledge, this is one of two Rough Rider Model 1883 shirts left in existence. The Tuttle shirt is currently on loan to the Arizona Historical Society in Tucson along with a recorded interview of Tuttle.

A second attributed shirt is that of Allen McCurdy of F Troop and is now in the collections of Ft. Sam Houston, San Antonio, Texas.

Since this cavalry regiment served in Cuba dismounted, their footwear unfortunately rose to a higher degree of need. Careful photographic study has yet to reveal the specific model shoe the Rough Riders were issued, as the canvas leggings cover the entire upper portion of the shoe itself, thus disguising any identifying construction feature. Nor has any attributed shoe from an enlisted man been located. What can be seen, however, is the lower section of the shoe, typical of the shoe or ankle boots worn throughout the army in the closing decade of the 19th century. Referred to as the "campaign shoe" by the quartermaster, models adopted in 1885, 1889, 1892 and 1893 all feature a heavy leather sole, a "ruffout" waxed upper dyed black, and finished with three hooks and from five to six eyelets all in brass.[8] The army made a serious effort to see that the average soldier was fitted with his particular size. For instance, the Model 1889 campaign shoe came in eight standard sizes with three different widths to each size.[9]

Due to the lack of unfavorable comments from the men, the campaign shoe seems to have given good service.

Perhaps more important to the soldier than the uniform itself are the undergarments he wears. As with the shoes, the exact type of these items issued to the Rough Riders is unknown to us. Underwear bottoms, or drawers as they were called, during this period, were commonly made of a cotton flannel, and reached to just above the ankle.

Model 1883 overshirt from the collections of AHS, Tucson. DWP

The issue undershirt adopted February 16, 1881 was made of a 50/50 mixture of cotton and wool, was long-sleeved and buttoned at the neck.[10]

Undoubtedly these undergarments were often lost, altered or discarded during the long summer campaign in Cuba, as extreme heat and the effects of dysentery took its toll on the troop's clothing.

The army also provided socks, referred to as stockings by the quartermaster, providing both cotton and wool socks.[11] Because of the utilitarian nature of socks, men returning from the war generally continued to wear them until discarded. This is referred to as "consumptive use of artifact."

Covering the tops of the ankle boot as well as the trouser just below the knee on the Rough Rider uniform were canvas leggings. They were made to fit close to the natural contour of the lower leg and matched the mid-brown color of the M-1884 fatigues, but a slightly heavier grade of canvas.

The pros and cons of leggings for foot soldiers (infantry), had been disputed by the army for many years. Those against the idea said it would make the foot too hot by keeping air from circulating, while others asserted they would prevent the fine powder-like dirt from entering the soldier's shoe on a long march, thereby keeping the foot healthier. For horse soldiers, it was thought that canvas leggings afforded the same protection as the old issue tall boot, but were lighter and more comfortable. After a period of experimental field trials in the mid-and late-1880s, the army adopted the canvas legging as part of the uniform. The infantry were given a 12-inch style, mounted troops were issued a taller 15 1/2-inch version.[12]

Quartermaster specifications for canvas leggings issued to mounted troops were to be made of 15-ounce cotton duck...and to be dyed a brown color...made in three numbered sizes, a No.1 being the smallest size, also varying in height, a No.1 being 14 1/2 inches tall, a

Original Model 1893 campaign shoe from the collections of AHS, Tucson. DWP

No.2, 15 1/2 inches and the largest, a No. 3 being 16 1/2 tall.[13]

Two sets of Model 1894 leggings with Rough Rider history are known to exist. *Please see figure 17 of the color plates and the back cover.*

No doubt the most practical and familiar item of the uniform given to the Rough Riders in San Antonio was their hat. The Model 1889 campaign hat was simple and modest in design, made of a drab fur felt body trimmed with an eight-ligne (grosgrain ribbon) union band with a 2 1/4-inch-wide leather sweat band. Each side of the hat was to have an opening for ventilation consisting of small punched holes (of a design similar to a snowflake). The brim to be 2 3/4 inches wide, front and rear and 3 inches at the sides finished with three rows of stitching at the edge.[14]

The campaign hat was issued in six numbered sizes, a No. 1 being a 6 3/4 and graduating in 1/8th inch intervals to a No. 6 in 7 3/8.[15]

The campaign hat of the Rough Riders became the signature of the American soldier at the time and fit the cowboy character of the regiment. *See figure 13 of the color plates.*

Already assembled in San Antonio, Texas, the Rough Riders donned their new uniforms on May 13. Non-commissioned officers' Model 1887 sleeve chevrons and trouser stripes of yellow facing cloth were sewn directly onto their brown canvas uniforms. Lt. Colonel Roosevelt was quite pleased with the unique appearance of his regiment and later wrote, "Their uniform suited them, in their slouch hats, blue flannel shirts, brown trouser, leggings, and boots. With handkerchiefs knotted loosely around their necks, they looked exactly as a body of cowboy cavalry should look.[16]"

---

[1] General Order No. 32, 16 April 1884.

[2] *U.S. Army Uniforms and Equipment*, 1889 by Quartermaster General of the Army, pages 58-59. Forward by Jerome A. Green, University of Nebraska Press.

[3] Ibid. pgs. 60-61.

[4] General Order No. 80, 17 Oct. 1888.

[5] Lt. Leonard Wood (Surgeon) "A Report on the Geronimo Campaign, 1886," Gatewood Collection, Arizona Historical Society, Tucson. "The uniform is totally unfit for service in Sonora or along our southern boarder...a cavalry soldier with heavy clothing clumsy boots is unable to do more than a portion of the work he can do perfectly dressed...."

[6] *U.S. Army Uniforms and Equipment*, 1889 by Quartermaster General of the Army, pages 56-57. Forward by Jerome A. Green, University of Nebraska Press..

[7] *Roosevelt's Rough Riders*, by Virgil Carrington Jones, pg. 35, Doubleday 1971. Excerpt from and Interview of Private Jesse D. Langdon of K Troop, "They issued us the damned blue woolen shirts that almost killed us with heat. I wore mine tied around my neck most of the time."

[8] *Boots & Shoes of the Frontier Soldier*, By Sidney B. Brinkerhoff. pgs. 23-24, 26-27, 29-30, 32, 1976 Museum Monograph No. 7, Arizona Historical Society,

[9] *U.S. Army Uniforms and Equipment*, 1889, by Quartermaster General of the Army, pgs. 300-302. Forward by Jerome A. Green, University of Nebraska Press.

[10] Ibid. pgs. 42-43.

[11] Ibid. pgs. 8 and 50.

[12] *Boots & Shoes of the Frontier Soldier,* by Sidney Brinkerhoff, pg. 35, 1976. Museum Monograph No. 7, Arizona Historical Society.

[13] *The Horse Soldiers, Vol. III*, By Randy Steffen, pg. 64. Notes on the Model 1894 leggings. University of Oklahoma Press.

[14] *U.S. Army Uniforms and Equipment*, 1889, by Quartermaster General of the Army, pg. 290. Forward by Jerome A. Green, University of Nebraska Press.

[15] *United States Army Headgear* 1855-1902, by Edgar M. Howell pages 60-61, Smithsonian Institution Press 1975.

[16] *The Rough Riders*, by Theodore Roosevelt, pg. 202 (New York: Scribners Sons, 1899).

Oliver B. Norton, left, and his brother, Sgt. Edward G. Norton, both of B Troop. The picture was taken in San Antonio. The younger brother, Oliver, was killed in the battle for Kettle Hill on July 1st. The older brother, Edward Norton, in Rough Rider sergeant's uniform with yellow Model 1887 cavalry chevrons and 1-inch trouser stripes. Note: Yellow (similar to the sergeant's stripes above) often photographed very dark in old black & white photographs. Edward is also sporting what appears to be a civilian hat. The canteen should be attached to the near side of the cantle. Image courtesy of PPLM.

Photograph identified as Sgt. Hunter, D Troop, Oklahoma Territory. Records indicated that there were two Sgt. Hunters from Oklahoma Territory in D Troop. His physical description matches most closely that of Charles E. Hunter, Enid, OT; Sgt. D Troop; 42, 5ft., 4 ins., ruddy, brown eyes, dark brown hair; born Guthrie; married. Image courtesy PPLN.

Khaki

During the first week in August new Model 1898 uniforms were given to the 1st Volunteer Cavalry in Cuba.[1] It had been over 12 weeks since the Model 1884 fatigues were handed out in San Antonio, and the constant heavy usage had reduced them to rags.[2] The men were directed to burn their "old clothes" as they had become unfit for service.[3]

This single act explains the rarity of the first issue uniform, and the relative abundance of 1898 uniforms attributed to the regiment. Study of Rough Rider photographs taken in September at Camp Wikoff strongly suggests that Troops C, H, I, and M left behind in Florida did not receive this new uniform. Seen are a good number of the men are still wearing their old fatigues. This seems logical as uniforms the men were wearing in Florida would not get the harsh treatment as those worn in Cuba. Troops A, B, D, E, F, K and L had greater need and received new clothing.

Human nature must also be taken into account as not all in Cuba actually destroyed their uniforms as ordered as in the case of Sgt. Palmer of D Troop. (Please see figures 4, 5, 6, 7 of the color plates.) His Model 1884 uniform is the only one of its kind. Luckily for us, the urge to take home his old uniform as a memento must have been too strong, and the order to burn it was disobeyed.

The new Model 1898 cavalry uniform for volunteer soldiers was quite a change from the simple brown fatigues. Adopted May 9, 1898 this new khaki outfit in some way resembled the British Army's uniform of the previous twenty years.[4] Made of a light cotton material, it featured a standing collar, 4 1/2-inch false pointed cuffs and shoulder tabs faced in the soldier's branch colors; light blue for infantry, red for artillery, and yellow for cavalry. The order also prescribed four large outside pockets with button closure on the coat, and khaki trousers and leggings to match.[5] (please see figures 18, 20, 21 of the color plates.)

The 1898 uniform order came too late for the army to build up sufficient stockpiles to issue before the Daiquiri landings. Having no suitable uniform for service in the tropics, the regular army went to war in its time-honored traditional blue uniform and in the case of the Rough Riders, the canvas fatigues.

The clean khaki uniforms with their yellow facing cloth and standing collars closely resembled the privately purchased dress which commissioned officers wore throughout the army. To their surprise, some of the Rough Riders received full military courtesy and even snappy salutes from enlisted men of other regiments. Some Spanish army officers also were fooled by the fine new uniforms. While on leave in Santiago, Private Arthur Tuttle of Safford, Arizona Territory, and some of his comrades were invited to drink with their Latin hosts (Spanish Officers) and former enemies. He later recalled, "they were real gentlemen."[6]

The army was shipped en masse to a detention camp at Montauk Point, Long Island, to recover from the effects of the Cuban campaign. The 1st Volunteer Cavalry were reunited there with the troops and horses left behind in Florida.

By mid-September, the Rough Riders were ready to be mustered out of service. Gone were the sharp-looking soldiers of three months before, when all were identically uniformed and military neatness was the order of the day. Now they were battle-scarred veterans, with depleted ranks to prove it. Cowboy boots and Stetson hats, along with an interesting mixture of old and new uniforms, could be seen--all worn at the whim of the individual. After all, they were a special bunch--they were the Rough Riders. And if the old cowboy adage is true, "A big hat does not a hand make," then it also can be said "A fine uniform does not a fighting man make."

---

[1] Rodger Fitch, G-Troop, *Personal Diary*, Rough Rider Museum Las Vegas, New Mexico. August 3, "New uniform with yellow cuffs, collars and shoulder straps issued this A.M. they look finely...."

[2] *The Rough Riders*, by Theodore Roosevelt, (New York Scribners Sons, 1899), pg. 202.

[3] Rodger Fitch, G-Troop, *Personal Diary*, Rough Rider Museum Las Vegas, New Mexico, August 7, "Busy in A.M. getting ready to move. Had a good wash and burned up my old clothes."

[4] J. Phillip Langellier, "From Blue Kersy to Khaki Drill *Military Collector and Historian*, Winter, 1982, pg 148.

[5] General Order No. 39, 9 May 1898.

[6] *Arizona Rough Riders*, by Charles Herner, Tucson, University of Arizona Press, 1970, pg. 178.

Pvt. William J. Pollack of D Troop. Photograph taken at Camp Wikoff, Long Island. Trooper Pollack is wearing his 1898 issue khaki uniform with yellow facings. Col. Roosevelt had this to say about Trooper Pollack's sense of humor... "One of the gamest fighters and best soldiers in the regiment was Pollock, a full blooded Pawnee. I never suspected him of having a sense of humor until one day, at the end of our stay in Cuba, as he was sitting in the Adjutant's tent working over the returns, there turned up a trooper of the First who had been acting as barber. Eyeing him with immovable face Pollock asked, in a guttural voice, 'Do you cut hair?' The man answered 'Yes' and Pollock continued, 'Then you'd better cut mine,' muttering, in an explanatory soliloquy, 'Don't wan't to wear my hair long like a wild Indian when I'm in civilized warfare." The pattern 1893 Godfrey modified saddle he is sitting upon clearly shows design flaws as the leather safe has moved up out of position and the quarter straps are too long. Page 21 ARIZONA ROUGH RIDERS by Theodore Roosevelt. Image courtesy HHLRC.

Letters from the McCurdy Brothers

Brothers F. Allen and J. Kirk McCurdy served with K Troop under the command of Cpt. Luna. During their enlistment in the Rough Riders, Allen and Kirk kept their father, J.M. McCurdy, informed through a correspondence of letters, many written at the front in Cuba.

The McCurdy letters contain a wealth of information on service in the Rough Riders, told in a matter-of-fact style, and through the eyes of two articulate and educated young soldiers.

After the war, the letters were printed in book form, titled *Two Rough Riders,* intended for private use. The following lines are excerpts taken from that book as they pertain to the subject matter of this book. The letters printed here are paraphrased, but as in their original form showing typographical errors and unique punctuation.

**On Board "Yucatan,"
Gulf of Mexico
June 15, 1898**

"...food is not so bad, and when one becomes used to it, it is quite good, and as our appetites are fine most anything tastes good. A meal consists of a large tin cup of coffee, corned or roast beef (canned), and either beans or tomatoes, sometimes both and all the hard tack we want.

With this regiment and on this boat there are two rapid fire and one dynamite gun, with crews from the Rough Riders."

Kirk

**Nine Miles from Santiago
June 25, 1898**

My Dear Father: - We landed at a small mining settlement Wednesday morning after the gunboats and *Indiana* had shelled the place for two hours.

Yesterday morning...ran into an ambush. The Spaniards were very strongly placed. Our troop had the extreme left of our advance skirmish line and with "L" troop (the extreme right) bore the brunt of the work.

In our fighting squad of ten men five were wounded (two mortally) and one killed; the man on my right was shot through the lungs and second man on my left was killed....

We lost everything, but after a long hunt yesterday afternoon and evening found all our things and are now comfortably fixed in our tent.

The marching is very hard work and we have dispensed with all unnecessary articles and cut our blankets to make our packs lighter.

Allen

**Near Santiago.
June 25 1898**

My Dear Father:
Ran into about four or five thousand Spaniards strongly place...our advance covered by their rapid fire gun on the distant hill.

I had my hat knocked off, also my bugle and haversack. I will keep these things as they are curiosities. We are both well and having a good time. When you write will you please enclosed some money as we have none and need it, as rations are scarce, an we need money for food.

Kirk

**Santiago nine Miles.
June 28, 1898**

My Dear Father:
...we marched five miles, and are now encampe nine miles from Santiago. This is a fine location for camp--water within a hundred yards and a good ope field free from brush for our tents.

Allen

June 28, 1898

Dearest Father:

Every day rations are issued consisting of a large slice of bacon and fat, two spoonfuls of sugar and the same of coffee, one tenth of a pound can of tomatoes and fifteen hardtack...

Those marches were pretty tough and lots of strong men gave out. Our load was pretty heavy. We carry our pajamas, underclothes and other articles rolled in a heavy blanket which is rolled in a half tent and covered by a rubber blanket; this goes over our shoulders. We have a carbine, one hundred rounds of ammunition in a belt, a canteen, a haversack with three days' rations (generally), and axe, pick or shovel, which is a pretty good load to carry four or five miles in the hot sun....

Kirk

Near Santiago.
June 29, 1898

My Dear Father:--We wrote you yesterday, but forgot to mention about our shoes. Will you please send us each a pair of heavy russet shoes? Kirk wishes his half a size larger than the last pair he bought from Miles, but I would like mine the same size. Do not send high boots, as they are too hot and heavy with our leggings over them. We have to wear leggings to protect ourselves from the heavy brush and thickets we travel through. Have leather strings put in, also several extra pair of strings and one tooth brush. The only way you can possibly get them here is by mail...please do not send us the clothes you said you would order, as we do not see them until we reach the States. The size of the leggings is No. 1 army leggings to match the cloth in the suit. The suit consists of trousers, leggings and blue army shirt. Kirk wishes trumpeter stripes on trousers (two stripes about one-eighth inch apart, stripes one quarter inch broad, and a yellow bugle on the blue shirt on each arm half way between the elbow and shoulder. Please have the clothes made and keep for us.

These are the same clothes we spoke to you about at Tampa. None of the men have coats and if you have not already ordered them do not do so.

Your loving son,
Allen.

June 29, 1898

Dearest Father:

...you had better send the shoes, as we will need them badly. If possible put a package of tea in each shoe, as it is quite a change from coffee; would be glad if you would send the shoes and undershirts (two apiece); no drawers, as we have them.

Your loving son,
Kirk.

P.S. - The leggings are cavalry leggings and reach about four inches below the knee.

Kirk.

Outskirts of Santiago, Cuba
July 7, 1898

My dear Father:

Last Thursday, June 30th, we broke camp and marched three miles to a block house near a large hill. There we camped over night, and the next morning the battle opened....we charged up the hill and the Spaniards retreated. Our loss was heavy, but we escaped without a scratch...Saturday we have been digging pits and making bomb proofs.

The day the battle opened we piled our stuff in the road and left a guard over it. He was hit by a pice of shell, and was taken out the hospital, and two days afterward when some of our troop went back, all our bundles had been opened, and most of our things stolen. We found two of Kirk's razors and a bundle of letters, which is all we have left except two University of Pennsylvania jerseys. We have since got hold of blankets and ponchos (rubber blankets), and are pretty comfortable.

Your loving son,
Allen

Santiago, Cuba
July 8, 1898

It is said the Spanish Volunteers have refused to go into their rifle pits, and the regulars are on the point of mutiny. Women and children have been coming through our lines for the last few days, and they say every house is filled with Spanish wounded and dead.

One of our troop who was sent back on an errand found our U. of P. jerseys and flag and our letters and diary, so we consider ourselves lucky, as most of the boys lost everything they had.

Your loving son,
Allen

Near Santiago.
July 8, 1898

My dearest Father:
As the Spaniards have violated most all international laws by firing on and killing Red Cross men carrying stretchers, and have used explosive bullets...Spaniards completely surrounded in, so there is no hope for them but to surrender.

Kirk

Santiago de Cuba
July 20, 1898

My dear Father:
After writing you several days ago, we broke camp and recamped on another part of the entrenchments three miles to the right. Sunday, 17th, the Spaniards stacked their arms and the American flag was raised over Santiago.

Seventy men left Tampa with our troop -- the other day at roll call thirty-eight reported for duty.

Allen

July 20, 1898

My dear Father: We have been looking every day for a letter from you but have not received any since leaving Tampa, although we have received several from Mr. Jamison and some girls.

The condition of the regiment is not good; yesterday there were one hundred and fifteen men on the sick report, which is not very good, as there are only about three hundred and fifty men in the regiment.

Kirk

Late variant of the Model 1898 cavalry tunic worn by Allen McCurdy. FSH - DBF

Near Santiago,
July 24, 1898

My own dear Father:-We had quite a surprise to-day when we received your very welcome letter, as it is the first that we have received from you since landing...the money was safe and we were really in need of it...and can buy many delicacies and some souvenirs also; but more important than all, clothes when we need them. For a day or so my shoes were pretty bad, but some one gave me a bag of tobacco, which I traded for a pair of shoes.

Our stomach bands have been worn night and day and I guess that accounts for our good health.

Allen

Near Santiago, Cuba
July 25, 1898

My dear Father: Yesterday was a most eventful day. We received a large amount of back mail...our regiment was supplied with fresh beef, the first we have tasted for over a month.

Dr. Church has given us several doses of quinine, which I think has been a great help in keeping us free from fever.

Tobacco has been very much in demand, and I saw a man pay five dollars for a small package. Last Sunday Kirk traded a small bag of "Durham" for a new pair of government shoes.

Captain Luna is on his staff as interpreter, and our troop is under Lieutenant Ferguson, of K troop.

Things are running smoother since the boats have been able to unload at Santiago, and we hope to get mail oftener. Yesterday we were ordered to floor our tents.

Woodbury Kane, lieutenant of K troop, is to-day the most popular man in camp. His sister sent the regiment a large box of tobacco and several cases of canned peaches.

The letter you enclosed us about our clothes mentioned "1st U.S. Cavalry." We will go over there to-day - they are camped near us - and make arrangements to have the box sent over there in case it miscarries and is taken to their camp. A great many letters miscarry; if not marked 1st Volunteer Cavalry, as the 1st Regular Cavalry is in our division.

Allen

**Near Santiago,
Santiago de Cuba,
Cuba.
July 26, 1898**

It would do you good to be here and see the mules; there are hundreds of them--great big flop-eared lanky simples, which carry big packs of eatables, about a hundred in a flock, without any rider or bridle, but they all follow a mare with a bell around her neck, and go in single file, like geese. There are about five men to a hundred mules, and they travel in this order everywhere, even carrying ammunition into the battle, where a good many are killed but they face the bullets like heroes.

By the way, this is Spanish paper and envelope I am writing on.

Kirk

**Near Santiago,
Cuba.
July 30, 1898**

My dear Father:--We have received in all twenty dollars from you, and thank you very much; for it is very useful in getting articles of food and clothing, which are to be had in Santiago... between the heat and the rain it keeps one in a perpetual drip; but it does not seem to hurt us as we are in fine health. The food now is much better; we get bread and fresh beef, potatoes, tomatoes and onions. Allen and I found a garden and had a good mess of corn and Lima beans, and now we often buy corn and beans from the Cubans, and so we live pretty well.

Kirk

**Santiago de Cuba
July 31, 1898**

My dear Father:

We still have some money left, as we only buy necessities. Shoes, stocking and blue top shirts were issued yesterday, and we expect our new uniforms and underwear in a few days.

Kirk

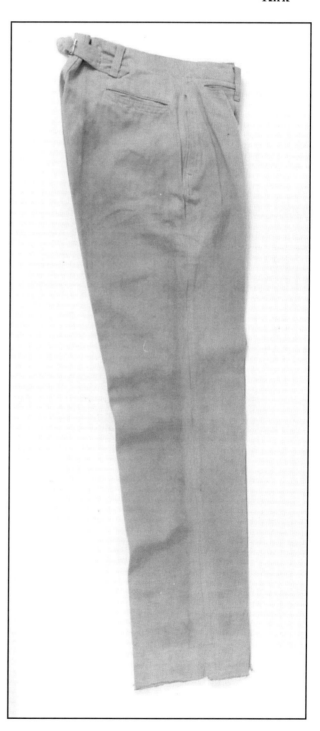

Model 1898 trousers, made of khaki drill from collections, AHS, Tucson. DWP

Excerpts from the Diary of F. Allen McCurdy

May 26th.--Telegram from Col. Roosevelt at 10 a.m. Left on 4:41 p.m. train for Washington.

May 29th.--Arrived San Antonio, Texas, 7:25 a.m. Examined and sworn in; bought uniform; reported at stock yard at 1 p.m.; assigned to Troop F, 2nd Squadron, Capt. Luna., in stockyard all afternoon and night.

May 30th.--Left for Tampa at 3:30 a.m.

June 3rd.--Arrived at Tampa and unloaded horses.

June 6th.--Camp. Slept on arms all night.

June 7th.--Paid off. Slept on R.R. tracks.

June 8th, 4 a.m.-- Left for Point Tampa in coal cars. Went aboard transport Yucatan No. 8, anchored in bay.

June 22nd.--Landed at S.A.I. Co.'s wharf twelve o'clock: small settlement called Daiquiri; fleet shelled the place and Spaniards left; Cubans arrived.

June 23rd.--Siboney; three days' rations; forced march of 10 miles.

June 24th.--Forced march. 5 a.m., battle Las Guasimas; drove Spaniards from ambush. 7-9 a.m., 60 men of regiment wounded and killed. 12 wounded, 1 killed, 2 mortally wounded in Troop F. Camped over night in battle ground. Assisted bringing in wounded and killed.

June 26th.--Marched five miles and camped within nine miles of Santiago. On guard; assisted capturing spies; had long talk with R. Harding Davis.

June 27th.--Outpost duty; assisted capturing spies.

June 30th.--Broke camp and moved three miles toward Santiago; stationed directly behind battery.

July 1st.--Battle opened 6:30 a.m. Fighting all day. Dug pits all night. Beginning of San Juan fight. Our troops suffered severely.

July 2nd.--Firing commenced at daylight: held position all day; brother had sunstroke; assisted carrying him off field to hospital.

July 3rd.--Spanish flag of truce raised 10 a.m.; digging trenches all day.

July 10th.--Sunday, out of trenches 4 a.m. 4:40 p.m. brother returned from hospital; commenced firing. Spaniards did not reply heavily.

July 17th.--American flag raised over Santiago at noon; rifle pits two hours. Spaniards stacked arms 11:45 a.m.

July 18th.--Changed camp; occupied Spanish block house on hill overlooking Santiago and harbor.

July 20th.--Brother in hospital. This is first time we had fresh beef since June 6th.

July 30st.--Blue Shirts and shoes issued.

July 31st.--Received two pairs stockings.

August 8th.--Sailed for Montauk.

August 12th.--Funeral at sea.

August 15th.--Landed at Montauk.

August 19th.--Ten days' furlough.

September 14th.--Mustered out at 5 p.m.

Group of Bronco Busters, Camp Wikoff, Long Island. As for the fighting spirit and attitude of the Cowboy Regiment, this photograph says it all. From left to right: Trooper William Wood, G Troop; Raton, N.M.; Alvin C. Ash, G Troop, Raton, N.M.; Thomas Darnell, H Troop, Deming, N.M.; Clay T. Owens, H Troop, El Paso, Texas; Newton Stewart, H Troop, El Paso, Texas; Augustus C. Fletcher, H Troop, Deming, N.M. All six cowboys seem to be stating their individuality in interpreting the Rough Rider uniform. Trooper Ash, 2nd from left, has removed the belt from his '98 coat and is wearing it as a trouser belt. Trooper Stewart is wearing sleeve garters and has returned to his cowboy boots. Trooper Fletcher, far right, is wearing a single set of USVs on his shirt collar, which was intended for the uniform coat. The first two troopers on the left from G Troop both show evidence of the new Model 1898 uniform issued in Cuba. The four men to their right, all from H Troop still retain their Model 1884 fatigues. (H Troop stayed behind in Florida.) Photograph courtesy HHLRC.

2nd Lt. Joshua D. Carter of A Troop in his Model 1895 officer's undress blouse. Visible are regulation false embroidered USV and Model 1895 crossed saber insignia, as well as 2nd Lt. cavalry shoulder boards. Photograph courtesy PPLM.

Officer's Uniforms

It was the accepted practice at the time of the Spanish American War that officers be responsible for acquiring their own uniforms and equipment at their expense.

Many established civilian firms such as Lilly, Horsemans, and Raymonds, catered to the needs of Army officers by offering everything from the latest in military dress to the finest in presentation quality swords. Another source for outfitting oneself in regulation attire was directly from the Army's Quartermaster Department.[1]

An officer at his garrison or post closely adhered to official dress "code" set down in Army regulations. Under the watchful eye of the post commander, strict obedience to proper dress was followed.

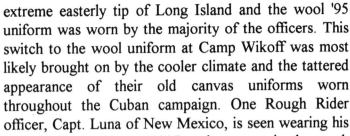
B Troop Capt. James McClintock's officers quality cartridge belt. Collections AHS Tucson. DWP

Campaign service, on the other hand, saw these high standards many times compromised. As an example, most of General Custer's officers at the "Little Big Horn" were outfitted in frontier buckskins and large white hats, including the general himself.[2] This habit of officers modifying or at times not wearing any part of the uniform at all on campaign could have come from their dissatisfaction with the uniform itself.

At the outbreak of war with Spain, a Model 1895 undress uniform was the authorized officer's service dress. The coat was single-breasted, made from dark blue cloth, with standing collar fastened with hook and eye, the coat to be trimmed with 1 1/4 lustrous black mohair flat braid as follows: all around the bottom, the front edges, the collar and both sides of the skirt openings.[3] The trousers were of light blue cloth, same shade of color as prescribed for enlisted men, with strips 1 1/2 inches wide, welted at edges, color that of facings of their respective arms.[4]

The prospect of having to wear a lined wool tunic and trousers while fighting an enemy during midsummer in the tropics could not have been very inviting.[5]

This Model 1895 tunic saw very limited use among Rough Rider officers during the hot summer months. By September the army was moved en masse to the extreme easterly tip of Long Island and the wool '95 uniform was worn by the majority of the officers. This switch to the wool uniform at Camp Wikoff was most likely brought on by the cooler climate and the tattered appearance of their old canvas uniforms worn throughout the Cuban campaign. One Rough Rider officer, Capt. Luna of New Mexico, is seen wearing his 1895 undress coat in the much printed (and famous) photographs taken on San Juan Hill. In July, while everyone else is in their shirts, this gentleman has every button done to the neck.

The decision to dress the enlisted men in an M-1884 fatigue uniform encompassed the officers as well. In a series of telegrams from Assistant Secretary of the Navy Theodore Roosevelt to Robert Ferguson of New York City, we find a clear intent to have everyone, officers and enlisted men, dressed in the same uniform.[6]

April 28, 1898

R.H.M. Ferguson, Esq.,
55 Liberty Street, New York.

Dear Bob:

I shall probably start next week. The officers will be elected by the men. I think you will get a commission in time, but I suppose you would behave to start in as a trooper like the others. Fifteen or twenty Harvard, Yale and Princeton boys are going. You will be given equipment and a horse, but you had better get your own uniform. Go to Brooks Brothers and get two suits of khaki like the one he is making for me; tan colored shoes and light leggings. Let me hear from you.

I shall detail you as my orderly if we can't do anything better for you. It is not necessary to say you should have a commission at once if I had the power; but I simply haven't the power.

Faithfully yours,
Theodore Roosevelt

In the next telegram sent to Ferguson, three days later, Roosevelt reverses his suggestion to get khaki uniforms and tells his friend he will dress in the same outfit as the enlisted men.

COWBOYS IN UNIFORM

Photograph of officers of 1st U.S. Volunteer Cavalry, San Antonio, Texas. As evidenced by this photograph, the lion's share of Rough Rider officers uniforms were altered Model 1884 fatigues. Two officers are wearing the prescribed Model 1895 officers undress coat are Lt. Hall, seated far right and Capt. Luna is standing behind Roosevelt's left shoulder. Six officers display the up-and-coming khaki uniform; Col. Wood, seated center; Lt. Col. Roosevelt, to his left; Maj. Dunn, to Roosevelts left; Lt. Sayre, standing at left, front row; Lt. Devereaux and Lt. Kane both standing back row. What is interesting is that only nine officers are seen wearing shoulder board insignia while some officers display no rank insignia at all other than 1 1/12-inch trouser stripes which for the most part are out of view. Major Brodie is holding the leash of the regimental mascot, an Arizona mountain lion named Josephine. Image courtesy SHM

May 1, 1898.
R.H.M. Ferguson, Esq.,
 55 Liberty St., New York.
My dear Bob:

I hated to have to telegraph you about having a canvas ordinary soldier's uniform instead of khaki, but it has proved impossible to get khaki uniforms in time, and I think it better for the gentlemen rankers that they should not be dressed differently from the other troopers.

I have written to your friend Taylor. Keep in touch with him and have him come on with you. Fifteen or twenty Harvard, Yale and Princeton fellows will be going. I may have to send you on ahead of me some time toward the end of this week, as I shall have to stay here until the end.

Faithfully yours,
Theodore Roosevelt

B Troop Capt. James McClintock's Model 1895 officers hat. AHS DWP.

Note: The two telegrams seen above and the one on page 63 are part of the Greenway Scrapbook kept at the Arizona Historical Society in Tucson.

A handful of Rough Rider officers did manage to acquire a khaki uniform in time. Col. Wood, Lt. Col. Roosevelt, Maj. Dunn and Lts. Kane, Sayre and Devereaux are all seen in San Antonio and Tampa photographs wearing khaki tan. Undoubtedly other officers had ordered khaki uniforms, but as Roosevelt pointed out in his second telegram to Ferguson, khaki was "impossible to get." Military clothiers and the quartermaster had no cloth with which to make the new uniforms.

Starting with the same basic Model 1884 uniform that the enlisted men were issued, the officers had them altered and no two seem to be alike. Yellow facing cloth was added and insignia appropriate to the wearer's rank was affixed along with U.S.V. insignia denoting they were the United States Volunteers, all done at the personal taste or available material of the individual.

Only the brown canvas coat of B Troop Capt. James McClintock has alone survived the years. Its survival as an artifact is largely due to the wounding of its owner on June 24, 1898 at Las Guasimas. McClintock was shot in the ankle while deploying his men on the firing line. The coat is a standard Model 1884, marked on the inside right breast with black ink, "Jeffersonville Depot" 189? Q.M. Dept. 4." The number four denotes the size of the coat. The collar has been cut down and faced with yellow wool. Seams on the cuffs have been opened and false pointed cuffs made from the same yellow wool have been sewn in. Cavalry Captain shoulder boards are attached. Two small eagle buttons have been added to the pockets while the six front buttons remain "as issued" India rubber.

Please see figure 8 of the color plates.

[1] *1895 U.S. Army Regulations, Clothing and Equipment*, page 167, paragraph No. 1198. Officers may purchase from the Quartermaster's Department such article of uniform, clothing, clothing materials and equipage as they need, provided the property is available. They will certify that the articles are from their personal use.
[2] *Boots & Saddles at the Little Big Horn*, by James S. Hutchins, page 15, Old Army Press, Ft. Collins, Colo. 1976.
[3] Regulations and notes for the uniform of the United States. 1889, Section No. 2.
[4] Ibid., Section No. 8.
[5] *Military Collector and Historian,* from "Blue Kersey to Khaki Drill," by J. Phillip Langellier, page 148, Winter 1982.
[6] *Roosevelt's Rough Riders,* by J.C. Jones, pg. 297. Doubleday and Company, New York, New York, 1971. "Ferguson, Robert Hector Munro, New York City; 2nd Lt. K Troop; joined May 5th Washington D.C.; sick in line of duty."

Officers' grouping taken at Tampa, Fla. A poor quality reproduction of an interesting photo. Cavalry sabers can be seen being carried by most of the officers. Gauntlets are in plain view. Gen. Joseph Wheeler is standing at right in light colored trousers with white beard with Col. Wood in khaki uniform at his side. Interesting to note, some officers have chosen to wear their saber belts underneath their fatigue coats. Image courtesy HHLRC.

Officers' photograph taken at Camp Wikoff, Long Island. Due to the cooler weather and poor condition of their old uniforms, most officers now wear the Model 1895 undress coat. Roosevelt and Surgeon Church, as well as others, are seen in their khaki uniforms. Standing at extreme left in civilian clothing is Lt. Horace K. Devereaux, wounded July 1st. Officers also appear to adopt some individuality in uniform, as evidenced by jodhpurs, leather leggings and boots. Photograph courtesy HHLRC.

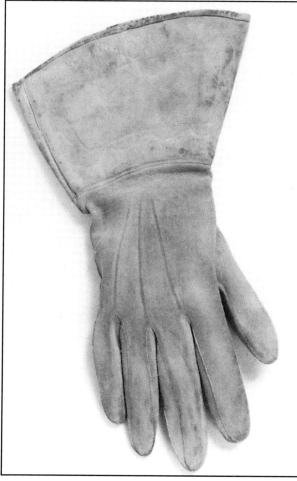

Wonder what they're laughing at? Wonderful photo taken at Camp Wikoff, Long Island, showing from left to right, Dr. Church, regimental surgeon; Charles Greenway; future President Col. Theodore Roosevelt, and at far right Pvt. Gordon Johnson, Roosevelt's mounted orderly. Dr. Church is wearing a khaki uniform with yellow facings and pocket flaps with elongated tongue shaped tabs. The horse he is holding by the on-side rein has an officer's style saddle cloth between the saddle and blanket. Greenway is seen sporting a Montana peak creased hat, a polka dot bandana and leather leggings with button closures. Since leaving Cuba, Col. Roosevelt decided to pin up the left brim of his hat and affixed the Model 1872 crossed sabers and a regimental No. 1. His gauntlets appear to be non-regulation with a much deeper than normal and exaggerated cuff segment. Plainly visible also are his officer quality saber belt and non-regulation leather leggings. Image courtesy HHLRC.

Left: Maj. Alexander Oswald Brodie's right handed gauntlet. Major Brodie was wounded in the right wrist at the Battle of Las Guasimas and obviously not wearing it at the time. Collections of SHM - DWP.

Accouterments

Ammunition for the 30/40 Caliber Krag Carbine was carried in the Model 1896 Mills & Orndorff Cavalry cartridge belt.[1] Made by the Anson Mills & T.C. Orndorff Company of Worcester, Massachusetts. This belt featured 50 double loops for .30-caliber ammunition and six double loops intended for the .38-caliber pistol for a total of 100 Krag and 12 pistol rounds. With some effort, .45 long colt rounds could be forced into the smaller .38-caliber loops, or simply used as additional loops for the .30-caliber Krag ammo.

The belt is made from a heavy dark blue webbing material, with all loops woven directly into the body, i.e. not sewn on or applied. The ends of the belt are captured or finished with a brass clamp and wire which serves as a means to adjust the belt to size. A large brass wire C closed the belt in front and acted as a buckle. Two 1/2-inch wide brass slides are found on each side of the belt ends.

On the bottom edge of the belt over the left hip is a brass wire loop and sabre hook held in place with a 1 inch leather chape and two brass rivets.

These cartridge belts, like the carbines, were in short supply. A man who was not issued with a cartridge belt probably did not get a carbine and lost his place in the invasion of Cuba to a man who did have them.

Ted Miller of D Troop found himself in just this sort of predicament. Only 69 members of his company were armed and equipped the night before going to Cuba. "I thought my goose was cooked," he wrote in his diary, "but I kept at it and hoped for something to turn up." Captain Huston of D Troop later approached Miller and handed him a gun and cartridge belt. "I asked no questions," Miller recorded, "but simply leaped inwardly at my good fortune. I learned afterward that a man had been asleep on guard the night before and they had taken his gun (and belt) and given it to me."[2]

Ted Miller was wounded in the neck July 1, 1898. Seven days later he succumbed to his wounds and died, July 8, 1898.[3]

Attached to the cartridge belt over the right hip a Rough Rider carried his .45-Colt revolver in a type 5 variant of the Model 1881 holster. Originally introduced in 1881 to fit the 7 1/2 inch barrel Colt, as well as the Smith and Wesson revolvers, this holster underwent a series of modifications to allow it to be carried with the ever wider belt designs used by the army.[4]

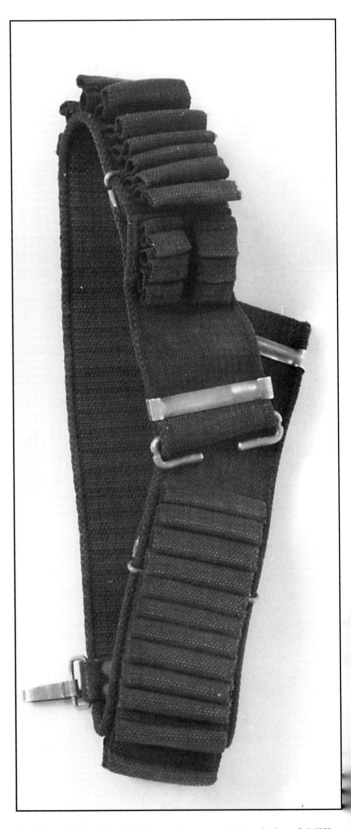

Original Model 1896 cavalry cartridge belt of Mills Orndorff patent. Author's collection. DWP

The type 5 variant holster is made with a shortened body segment to accommodate the 5 1/2-inch barrel (artillery model) Colt single action revolver. It also had a much larger frog (belt loop) to fit over the double loop (Krag) cartridge belt then in use.

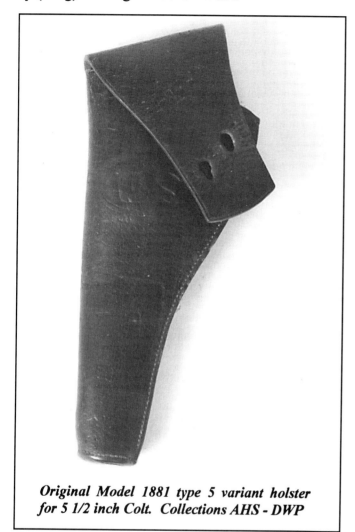

Original Model 1881 type 5 variant holster for 5 1/2 inch Colt. Collections AHS - DWP

The holster is made from 8 1/2 to 9-ounce leather dyed black, fashioned with a toe plug sewn in at the bottom, a flap to hold the pistol in place, closed with a brass stud, a belt frog, and the letters "U.S." surrounded by an oval stamped in front.[5]

It is doubtful many of these holsters were taken to Cuba as the Colt side arms were taken away just prior to leaving for Port Tampa.

Two items of equipment given to a Rough Rider that, at a glance, instantly identified him as a horsesoldier were his spurs and gauntlets.

These also were cavalry equipments and were left behind with the horses in Florida as they would soon lose their usefulness while soldiers were struggling up a jungle trail in Cuba on foot. It was also against regulations to wear spurs on dismounted duty.[6]

Gauntlets though, might come in handy in the thick underbrush, and some were taken.

The issue spur in 1898 was the Model 1885, made of cast brass with a 3/4 inch bar loop on each side for spur straps, with steel rowels 27/32 diameter. The straps were made of 7-8 ounce leather, with brass wire buckles and leather standing loops.[7]

Specifications for leather gauntlets were: to be made of Angora goat skin, cuffs to be at least 4 1/2-inches deep....and to be lined with Russet leather...and to be made in five sizes.[8]

Surviving gauntlets with Rough Riders attribution are as follows: single right hand gauntlet belonging to Major Alexander O. Brodie, wounded in the right wrist at the battle of Las Guasimas, in the collections of the Sharlot Hall Museum, Prescott, Arizona; a complete pair once owned by C Troop Capt. Joseph Alexander now in the collections of A.H.S., Tucson. *(Please see figure 19 of the color plates.)*

An article of great importance to a soldier at this time was the haversack. In it he carried all his eating utensils, food, and all small items he deemed necessary to his comfort and survival.

The haversack was not part of the original equipment issue given out in San Antonio, but was issued to the men only when their horse gear and side arms were packed up and handed in after they were ordered to Cuba dismounted. Prior to that time, they used the saddle bags.

An attributed haversack and sling with Rough Riders provenience belongs to the Sharlot Hall Museum, Prescott, Arizona. Once carried by B Troop Pvt. Jackson Harvey Misner, a 24-year-old locomotive fireman from Bisbee, Arizona Territory.[9] (Please see figure 15 of the color plates).

The Misner haversack is of the Model 1878 pattern made at Rock Island arsenal. Made entirely of drab duck and webbing, it features a large double thickness flap marked with the letters "U.S." 1 1/2 inches tall, in black with a 3/4-inch wide by eight-inch long strap attached to the bottom. The body was constructed with an inside pocket sewn into the back seam and a meat-can pocket sewn in the front. There are also two side pockets to accommodate the knife, fork and spoon. The sling is made of 7-8 ounce black collar leather, 2 inches wide in the middle and tapering to 1 1/8-inch wide ends. Length is adjusted by two brass wire hooks and five holes, punched into the leather on each end.

The Rough Riders mention their haversack many times in letters, diaries, and in reminiscing. Lt. Tom Rynning of B Troop reported in his book *Gun Notches*, "We was the worst starved-out bunch for three days after the Guasimas run in that ever happened, when we went into action at Guasimas, we piled all our haversacks in a heap, and while we was fighting the Spaniards, the lousy Cuban Soldiers came along and stole every bit of grub out of them."[10] Roger Fitch of G Troop went on to relate in his diary "June 26...very warm. (Private William) Cody, my 'bunkie' (a distant relative of 'Buffalo Bill') and I have but one haversack between us and so take turns carrying it."[11] Also read Allen McCurdy's letter of July 7, 1898 on page 12.

The contents of the haversack varied with individual soldiers, but usually contained the following articles: the Model 1874 (type 3) meat can, a two-piece outfit made of sheet steel, and tin-washed device consisting of an iron handled pan, and small plate made to fit within the overlapping lip of the pan.[12] Carried in the front-most pocket of the haversack. Stored in the two small side pockets are the eating utensils of the 1874 pattern. The knife measured 9 inches overall with a 5 1/4-inch pointed blade and "U.S." stamped on the left. The three-tine fork measured 7 1/2 inches overall. Both knife and fork are made of steel with cast iron handles painted black; each has its own leather scabbards so as not to damage the haversack. The 7 1/2 inch spoon is heavy cast iron tin washed with "U.S." stamped into the handle. The army also issued small cloth bags for salt, sugar and ever-important coffee.

Without a doubt, the most valuable piece of equipment carried by soldiers during the hot months in Cuba was the canteen. At the close of the Civil War; in 1865, the Quartermasters Department had on hand a vast supply of material, among it, canteens. These stockpiles of existing canteens were altered over the next three decades by changing the coverings and methods of suspension.

By 1898 the last surplus of Civil War canteen bodies were still being issued to U.S. troops. New production of canteens resumed during the Spanish American War and can be identified by a sheet rolled neck in contrast to the cast pewter necks of the 1858 model. The canteens used by the 1st U.S. Volunteer Cavalry were Model 1858 canteens altered to the current specifications by removing the old covers, corks, straps and three tin standing loops. Two triangular steel loops were added by means of soldering tin straps to the right and left seams of the body. They were covered first with Grey Petersham and an out cover of drab duck. A 1 1/2-inch "U.S." was stenciled on the side. The cork was attached to the canteen by a 3-inch long flat, brass chain and ring closed around the neck of the mouth-piece. Although the infantry used

Original Model 1878 haversack held open to reveal inner pockets. Photograph courtesy author's collections and DWP

long leather shoulder strap, the mounted service received a strap made of 7 to 8-ounce leather with an iron roller buckle and two sliding loops and one standing loop. One snap hook was attached to a leather loop which was movable along the doubled strap for attachment to a ring on a saddle or to a loop on a cartridge belt.[14]

The author has examined two canteens once carried by Rough Riders, the first belonging to G Troop Pvt. William C. Gibson, a 24-year-old New Mexican from Gallup. Gibson's canteen is marked on the opposite side from the "U.S." stamp with the hand-written initials "W.C.G."

The second canteen was used by Private Hopping. Please see photograph on back cover.

The issue tin cup for the Rough Riders is the Model 1874, measuring, on average, 4 inches in diameter by 4 1/8 inches high. It was made of "XXXX" block tin with a rolled lip and flat-crimped bottom affixed by a wiped solder joint. A folded and soldered seam extended up the side under the handle. The small ear-shaped handle measured 1 1/8 inches wide at the top and 5/8-inch wide at the bottom. It was fastened to the side of the cup by two roundheaded iron rivets at the top and one at the lower end. Stamped in the handle were the letters "U.S." 3/8-inch high.[15] A cup of this kind was carried by Oscar G. Wager of A Troop, a cowboy from Jerome, Arizona Territory. The cup itself was pierced by a Spanish bullet during the fighting in Cuba. See photo on back cover.

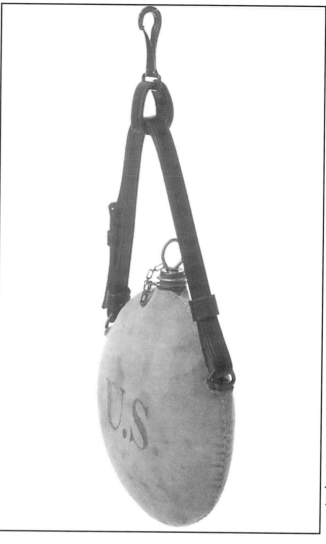

Original model 1885/1898 canteen with reproduction cavalry hanger. Authors collection. DWP

Beginning in 1896, canvas breech covers were issued on a trial basis. By 1897 more than 16,000 were in use by the army.[16] A simple three-piece sewn canvas duck cover with two leather thongs attached, front and back. Its main function was to keep the gun's mechanism free from dirt and water. The device was secured to the gun by placing the fitted contoured areas over the intended parts of the gun breech, then

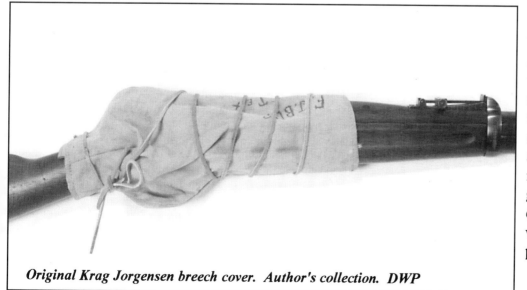

Original Krag Jorgensen breech cover. Author's collection. DWP

Original abdominal stomach bandage or wrap. Author's collections. DWP

wrapping the thongs around until they met, and tying a knot. The two original covers in the author's collection are both marked the same. Stamped on the inside in black ink are the words, "ROCK ISLAND ARSENAL" and "PLACE OVER COCKING PIECE."

It is doubtful that many of these covers actually saw use among the Rough Riders, though some troopers improvised and fashioned their own covers (see photographs on pages 59 and 61). The M-1896 breech covers are discussed here for that reason alone.

An odd but interesting apparatus in use during the Spanish American War was the abdominal bandage made of a light grey wool flannel cloth measuring 40 by 8 inches and tied in back by four 1/2 inch cotton strings. Its purpose when worn was to keep the skin on the stomach area warm in hot weather. It's hard to imagine someone wearing one of these tied around his middle during a tropical midsummer campaign in Cuba while the body is struggling to cool itself. The medical ideas of that period seem like so much quackery today. I believe this is the stomach band McCurdy is referring to in his letter dated July 24, 1898. (See page 13.)

[1] Note: though referred to as the M-1894 or later "cavalry mills belt" by collectors. This particular model belt most likely wasn't adopted or seen until 1896, as there were no carbines issued until that year.
[2] *Roosevelt's Rough Riders*, by Virgil Carrington Jones. Pages 62, 63, Doubleday, 1971.
[3] *The Rough Riders*, by Theodore Roosevelt, pg. 248, New York, Scribners & Sons, 1899.
[4] *Packing Iron*, by Richard Rattenbury, pg. 31, Zon International, Millood, N.Y. 1993.
[5] *Ordinance Memoranda, No. 29*, Introduction by James S Jutchins, Page 50. Westernlore Press, Tucson, AZ 1984.
[6] *Cavalry Drill Regulations*, 1896, War Department, Document No. 14, Section 62.
[7] Ibid. *Ordinance Memoranda No. 29*, pg. 41.
[8] *U.S. Army Uniforms and Equipment*, 1889, by Quartermaster of the Army, pg. 130, Forward by Jerome A Green, University of Nebraska Press.
[9] Ibid. *Roosevelt's Rough Riders*, page 317.
[10] *The Arizona Rough Riders*, by Charles Herner, Tucson University of Arizona Press, 1970, pg. 115.
[11] *Roger Fitch, G Troop Personal Diary*, Rough Rider Museum Las Vegas, New Mexico.
[12] *The U.S. Army in the West 1870-1880*, by Douglas C McChristian. Pg. 213, University of Oklahoma Press, 1995.
[13] Ibid, pg. 215.
[14] *Ordinance Memoranda, No. 29*, Introduction by James S Jutchins, Page 52. Westernlore Press, Tucson, AZ 1984.
[15] Ibid., *U.S. Army in the West 1870-1880*, pg. 214.
[16] *The Krag Rifle*, by Lt. Col. William S. Brophy, pgs. 161-162 The Gun Room Press, Highland Park, N.J. 1995

COWBOYS IN UNIFORM

Figure 1. A recreated scene of typical 1st U.S. Volunteer Cavalry uniforms circa 1898. From left to right, company captain wearing altered Model 1884 fatigues, showing yellow facing on collar and cuffs. 1 1/2-inch-wide cavalry officer's striping on trousers and appropriate shoulder insignia; lieutenant colonel wearing custom tailored officer's uniform from Brooks Brothers clothiers of New York, New York. Both captain and lieutenant colonel wear false embroidered U.S.V. and crossed saber insignia on their collars. Please note Lt. Colonel has chosen not to include shoulder insignia denoting rank or stripes on his trousers. Company guidon sergeant. in 1884 fatigue uniform with Model 1887 trouser stripes and sergeant's chevrons applied. He is holding a troop guidon attached to a 9-foot lance. Private in 1884 fatigue uniform unadorned with army rank or insignia, holding a Model 1896 Krag Jorgenson carbine. Both private and sergeant wear Model 1896 Mills cavalry model cartridge belt with side arm attached. Photo courtesy DWP.

Figure 2. A recreated scene of an enlisted Rough Rider being issued his equipment. Figure at left seems somewhat mystified by the actual function of the Model 1885 surcingle he is holding. Sergeant at right, perhaps a veteran, is instructing him on its intended use. Also visible in the scene is the trooper's new Godfrey converted saddle with saddle bags, canteen and carbine attached. The sergeant is holding Model 1874 curb bridle and 1885 halter. Visible on the ground is an 1885 horse hair cinch, tin cup, bed blanket, saddle blanket and rubber poncho. Photography DWP

Figure 3. Having received orders to act as dismounted cavalry, Rough Riders are preparing their equipment to leave camp and board transport for the invasion of Cuba. Sergeant sitting at left is filling his cartridge belt for the first time with tin washed Frankfort Arsenal ammunition. Trooper kneeling has rolled his curb bridle, horse brush and comb inside his saddle blanket and is attaching it to the cantle of his saddle. He has already taken what he needs out of the saddle bags and transferred the contents into his haversack lying on his blanket roll, just in front of the sergeant. Cavalry officer is watching, instructing. Recreated scene. Photo courtesy DWP

Figures 4 & 5. Original Model 1884 fatigue coat belonging to Orlando G. Palmer of Ponca City, Oklahoma Territory, 1st Sgt. D Troop, 1st U.S. Volunteer Cavalry. This coat and trousers pictured on the next page are the only Model 1884 enlisted man's fatigues known to have survived to date with Rough Rider attribution. Photo courtesy DBP.

Figures 6 & 7. Model 1884 trousers belonging to Sgt. Palmer, D Troop. These trousers appear to have been heavily worn. Visible are the 1-inch yellow wool Sergeant's stripes applied to the outside seam. This remarkable uniform can be seen on display at Fort Sam Houston, San Antonio, Texas. Photo courtesy DBP

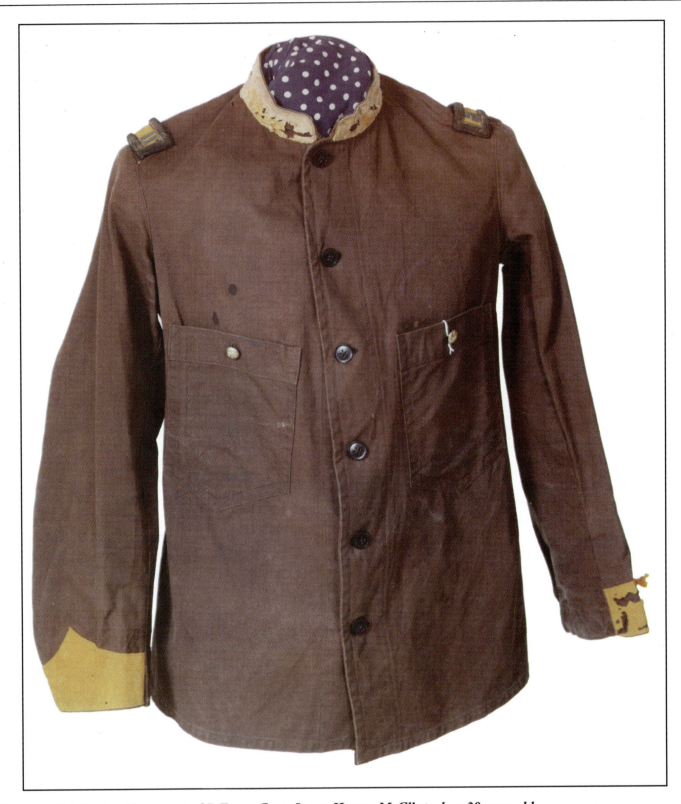

Figure 8. Original uniform coat of B Troop Capt. James Harvey McClintock, a 38-year-old newspaperman from Phoenix, Arizona Territory. Capt. McClintock was wounded by two Mauser hits above the left ankle while deploying his men during the battle of Las Guasimas, June 24, 1898, at which time 1st Lt. George Wilcox assumed command of the troop. This Model 1884 coat altered to officer's use is the only one of its kind located by the author. The coat shows much of the original brown color of the 1884 fatigues, unlike the washed out uniform of Sgt. Palmer on pages 31 and 32. This coat is currently on exhibit at the Arizona Historical Society, Tucson. DWP

Figure 9, above, officer's quality coat belonging to C Troop Capt. Joseph Alexander, a 40-year-old lawyer from Phoenix, Arizona Territory. Capt. Alexander began service in the Rough Riders as B Troop's first lieutenant. When the regiment was authorized to be expanded, Alexander received his captain's bars and his own company command. Inset, right, Figure 10: Detail of Capt. Alexander's coat showing unfaded portion of uniform under breast pocket flap. Photo courtesy DWP. Artifact courtesy collections Arizona Historical Society, Tucson, Arizona.

COWBOYS IN UNIFORM

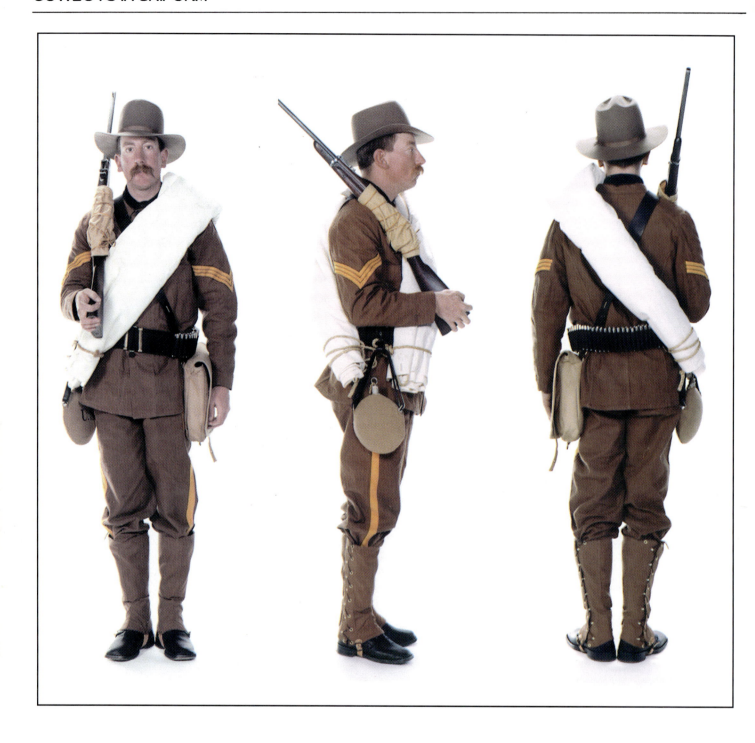

The fully outfitted Rough Rider

Figure 11. Recreated scene of Rough Rider non-commissioned officer appearing ready to board transport for the invasion of Cuba. His spurs have been removed, most likely packed away with his saddle equipments. His Colt revolver and holster were returned for safekeeping. He has transferred all the contents of his saddle bags into his haversack that hangs from his left hip. His change of underclothing, rubber poncho, and bed blanket are rolled into his shelter tent which rests on his left shoulder. His canteen filled with water is hanging by the snap hook from the cartridge belt. His tin cup is not shown as it was mislaid. This sergeant has managed to acquire the proper Model 1886 breech cover for his carbine. Photo courtesy DWP

COWBOYS IN UNIFORM

Figure 12. Recreated scene of soldiers examining captured Spanish weapons. Soldier at left depicts a non-commissioned officer of the regular army wearing mid-blue wool trousers with 1 inch sergeant's stripes in the branch color of white for infantry. His Mills cartridge belt is of the infantry pattern, having no pistol ammunition loops or saber hanger. The campaign hat, shoes, leggings and shirt are the same as worn by the Rough Rider private standing left except for the crossed rifle infantry insignia pinned to his hat. He is holding a Model 1896 Krag rifle. In his left hand is a .43 caliber Spanish Remington Rolling Block rifle with bayonet. The Rough Rider private examines the rifle bore of a captured Model 1893 Spanish Mauser. Photo courtesy DWP.

COWBOYS IN UNIFORM

Figure 13. Pictured above is an original Model 1889 campaign hat belonging to hospital steward James B. Brady, 1st U.S. Volunteer Cavalry, 1898. Model 1872 enlisted man's crossed saber insignia and regimental No. 1 attached. Collections Sharlot Hall Museum. Photograph DWP   Figure 14. Pictured left an original pair of Model 1887 suspenders. Collections Hayes Otoupalik. Photograph DWP

Figure 15. Grouping of haversack and contents. Tin-plated iron spoon, round hardcracker and haversack carried by Pvt. Jackson Harvey Misner of B Troop, a locomotive fireman form Bisbee Arizona Territory. Mess tin used by hospital steward James Brady. Scratched on the surface of the tin is "J.B.B. J.B. Brady B." All of the above from the collections of SHM. Original soldier's drinking cup from the collections of Michael L. Woodcock; original issue knife and fork resting on their individual leather scabbards. Author's collection. DWP

Figure 16. Recreated scene of Rough Rider sergeant in action in Cuba 1898. Having already taken off his haversack and blanket roll and left them piled up with others from his company and keeping only his canteen and cartridge belt, he is now ready to confront the Spanish. He has chosen to load his carbine one at a time from the belt and keep the magazine full as a backup. DWP

Figure 17. Above: Original dark brown Model 1894 leggings belonging to C Troop Capt. Joseph Alexander.
Figure 18. Right: Original Model 1898 leggings, also once worn by Capt. Alexander. Both sets of leggings are from the collection of the AHS, Tucson. DWP

Figure 19. Original cavalry gauntlets once owned by Capt. Alexander. These gauntlets and the leggings seen in figures 17 & 18 on the previous page all belonged to the same soldier. Being the captain of C Troop, he did not take part in the Cuban campaign, which might account for the artifacts' excellent condition. Collections AHS. DWP

Figures 20, 21. Original Model 1898 uniform coat belonging to Pvt. Charles O. Hopping, F Troop, 1st U. S. Volunteer Cavalry 1898. This is a textbook example of the first or early variant of the Model 1898 uniform. With slanting pockets faced in yellow, this coat has false embroidered brass USV letters attached to the collar; the belt is also detachable. This coat is one of five identical Model 1898 coats at the Rough Rider Museum in Las Vegas, N.M. The other four uniform coats are attributed to Pvt. Bernard of K Troop, Pvt. Lisk and Trumpeter Bell of F Troop and Pvt. Ludy of E Troop. DWP

COWBOYS IN UNIFORM

The artifacts photographed on this page are the uniform and items brought home by James Brady who served as a hospital steward with the 1st U.S. Volunteer Cavalry 1898. Pictured above is his coat with hospital sergeant's chevrons on each arm. Due to the overall fine quality, added yellow cloth over the lower pockets and deeper color of facing cloth, the author believes this coat is custom made, i.e. not issue. Pictured below are Brady's Model 1898 trousers with 1 1/4-inch-wide green stripes (sergeant's stripes should be 1-inch wide). Also seen are his hospital brassard (arm band), a Johnson & Johnson bandage, a tourniquet and a whiskey flask, showing the effects of a .07x.57-caliber Spanish bullet entering one side of the flask only. The bullet has been removed from the flask and is lying nearby. This rare Rough Rider grouping is in the collections of the SHM. DWP

Original photograph of Hospital Steward Brady standing behind one of the hospital tents at Camp Wikoff, Long Island, New York. Brady's uniform and other items attributed to him can be seen on page 43. Image courtesy HHLRC.

Weapons

As previously referred to in the introduction of this book, Col. Wood thought it imperative that the 1st U.S. Volunteer Cavalry get equipped and trained quickly. He also knew that if the regiment was to see any combat at all they must have modern weapons.

Roosevelt had this to say about his commanders goal, "Wood thoroughly realized what the Ordnance Department failed to realize, namely the inestimable advantage of smokeless powder; and, more over, he was bent upon our having the weapons of the regulars, for this meant that we would be brigaded with them, and it was evident that they would do the bulk of the fighting if the war were short. Accordingly, by acting with the utmost vigor and promptness, he succeeded in getting our regiment armed with the Krag-Jorgensen carbine used by the regular cavalry." [1]

In Wood's mind having the regiment armed with obsolete .45/.70 caliber Trapdoor Springfields meant that if they got to Cuba at all they would be relegated to guarding supplies on the beach, or worse, occupying Cuba after the fighting was over; either was unthinkable to him.

In the last decades of the nineteenth century many European countries adopted small caliber cartridge and magazine long arms for military use. These flatter shooting, higher velocity weapons were far superior to the heavy large caliber rifles then in service with the U.S. military.[2]

On November 24, 1890, General Order No. 136 was issued by U.S. Army Headquarters. The order appointed a board of officers and directed them to supervise and conduct tests, then to make a recommendation on a suitable selection of a new magazine arm and cartridge.[3] On August 19, 1892, the Office of the Board on Magazine Arms made their choice. The Krag- Jorgenson was found" to be vastly superior for use in the United States Service....."[4] Invented by Col. Ole Krag and Eric Jorgenson of Norway and adopted by Denmark in 1889 and by Norway in 1894, the Krag-Jorgensen design proved accurate and reliable and was even used by Norwegians during WW II to resist the invading German army.[5]

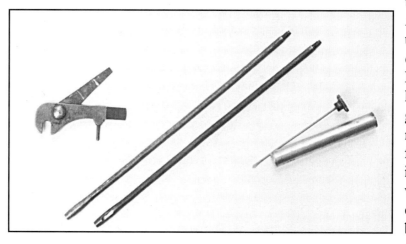

Model 1879 rifle tool and 2- piece sectional cleaning rod with oiler carried in the stock of the Krag carbine. Author's collections.

Simply referred to as the Krag by most American collectors, its unique appearance is quickly recognized. Featuring a bottom hinged box magazine gate or door on the right side, rounds are fed or dropped in. Thus it can be reloaded without clearing the chamber, i.e. pulling the bolt back. By utilizing a cut-off lever on the left side the ammunition in the magazine can be held in reserve and the weapon used as a single shot. The Krag design suffered in comparison with the Model 1893 Mauser rifle used by the Spanish in two areas. First, the Mauser 7x57 cartridge performed better. The higher muzzle velocity of the Spanish rifle allowed it to be more accurate. Also, rounds were fed into the magazine much quicker by way of a striper clip, as compared to loading one at a time from a cartridge belt as the Krag system required.

Springfield Armory went into full production of the Krag rifle, Infantry model, in 1894.[6] The Model 1896 carbine was approved May 23, 1895; the first issue of the weapon to troops began March 10, 1896. By May of the year, all ten regiments of the regular cavalry were armed with the new Krag.[7] Approximately 20,000 Model 96 carbines were produced at Springfield Armory; some estimates say over 22,000 were made.

The .30-40 Krag cartridge had the distinction of being the first smokeless powder rifle round adopted for use in the U.S., military or civilian market.

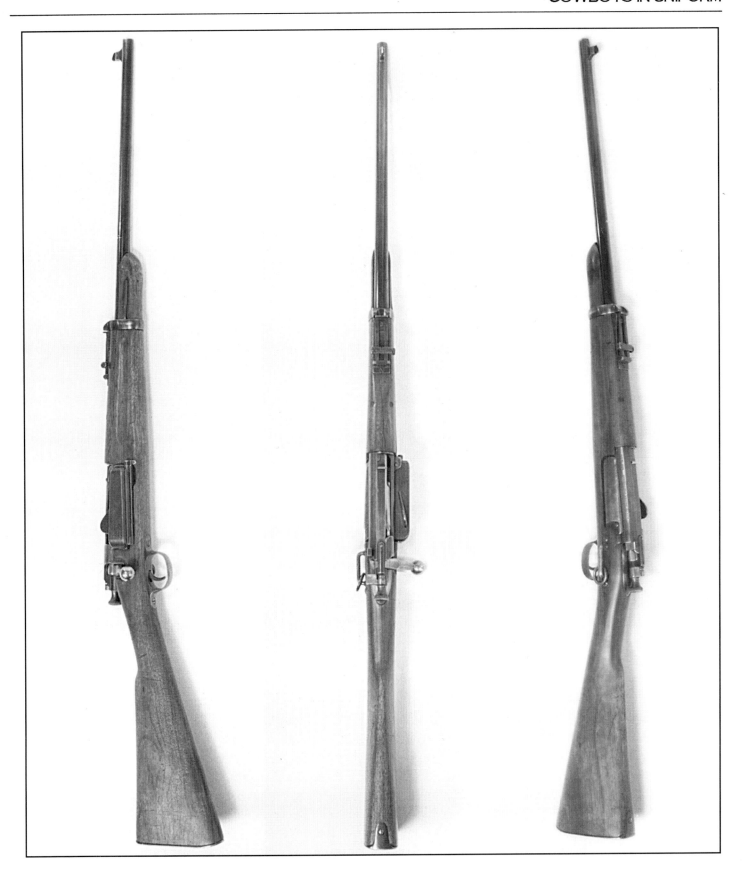

Original Krag Jorgenson Model 1896 carbine. Author's collections. DWP

Original photograph identified as Rough Riders from G & I Troops, taken May 16, 1898 at San Antonio, Texas. It is interesting to note that not all of the troopers have the proper Mills-Orndorff cartridge belt or holsters for their Colt revolvers. It is likely that these supply shortages were remedied by the time the regiment received orders for Tampa 13 days later on May 29. Officer on extreme right with arms folded has chosen to wear his saber belt underneath his fatigue coat in a way that mimics the Model 1895 officers coat. Image courtesy MNM.

Production of standard ball ammunition for the military was at Frankford Arsenal. Muzzle velocity of the service round with a 220 grain bullet, fired from a 30-inch rifle barrel was 2,000 feet per second, much faster than the old .45-70 black powder round at 1,350 f.p.s.[8]

In an effort to preserve the once fired cartridge case for reloading, early Krag ammunition had a tinned case and had a silver appearance. This Fankford Arsenal practice of tinning the case was discontinued after May 1900.[9]

Early Model 1896 Krag carbine receivers made during the year 1895 carry that date stamped into the left side of the receiver itself. Even though they are true Model 1896 carbines, they will be stamped 1895 instead of 1896. In an informative article entitled "Guns of the Rough Riders" for the *Man At Arms*, January/February 1989 publication, author Frank Mallory had this to say about the serial numbers from G & I Troop carbines,".... their carbines fall into several fairly well defined ranges. If the numbers (from G & I Troops) comprise a valid sample, most of the Rough Rider carbines were from the lot manufactured in 1895 and completed in 1896; these (serial numbers in the 20,000 range) will all have the 1895 receiver marking." Mr. Mallory went on to say, "As I have noted in my serial number books and elsewhere, these arms were not issued in serial number order, so you cannot assume that a carbine number consecutive with one of the Rough Rider arms would also have been used by that illustrious unit." Accompanying this article was a listing of Rough Riders from G & I troops with the serial number of the carbine issued them. The numbers observed in these two troops ranged between 26784 and 79499 with the majority falling in the 28xxx range.

It is my belief that only a few attributed Rough Rider carbines may ever be found as they were returned to government stores or, due to hard service, sent back to the Arsenal for refitting. The odds of locating more identified carbines would improve with the rest of the troop issue serial numbers from the regiment.

The service handgun for the U.S. Army at this time was the new Colt double action model 1892 revolver in .38 caliber (.38 long Colt). During the war with Spain and especially the Philippine Insurrection, the Army found the .38 long Colt had insufficient stopping power for combat use, and was discontinued in 1911.[10]

Undoubtedly many Rough Rider officers carried the .38 Colt double action. L Troop Captain Allyn Capron's .38 D.A. is now kept at the Smithsonian Institution along with other items once owned by the brave career soldier killed at the Las Guasimas fight.[11]

Roosevelt also used a .38 D.A. in Cuba. His particular revolver was salvaged from the Maine wreck that sank in Havana Harbor. Roosevelt's brother-in-law, W.S. Cowles U.S.N., gained possession of it and presented it to T.R.[12] The serial number of this historic pistol is #16334. Engraved on the left side

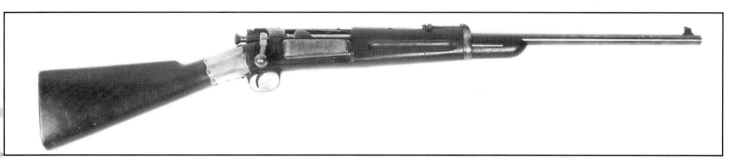

Top: Original Model 1896 carbine brought home by Lt. Greenway. 2nd from top: Closeup of the left side of the Greenway carbine reveals arsenal stamping as follows: "1895 U.S. Springfield, Armory. 28135." Records indicate this weapon was issued to J. Knox Green of G Troop. Trooper Green died August 15 of sickness at Montauk Point.

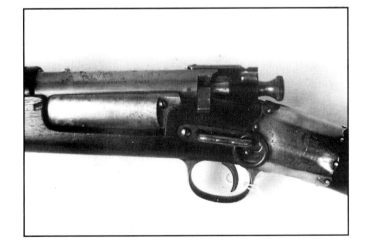

Above: Right side of Greenway carbine detailing silver plaque that reads "Las Quasimas Kettle Hill San Juan." Left side of Greenway carbine detailing silver plaque that reads "Lt. John C. Greenway Roosevelt's Rough Riders." This attributed carbine is shown here through the courtesy of AHS Tucson. DWP

An original photo of Trooper William Owens, B Troop, nicknamed "Smoke 'em up Bill" by his comrades after a shooting incident in San Antonio. Trooper Owens has chosen to move his carbine and holster to the "on" side of his horse, so as to display his weapons for the photographer. Note that there is no ammunition in his belt. He is properly mounted on a sorrel of B Troop. Image courtesy PPLM.

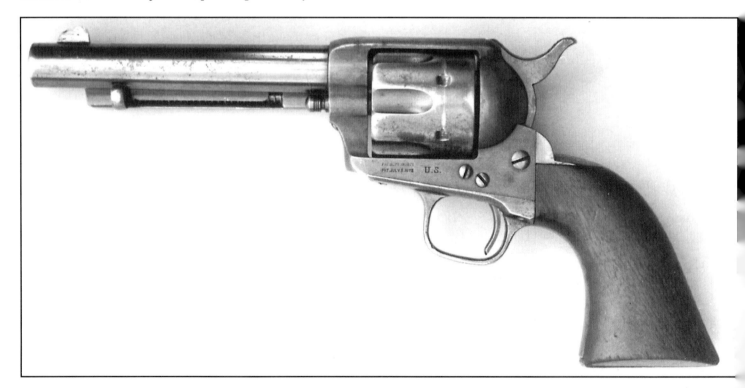

Original short barrelled Colt revolver in .45 caliber. Plainly visible are the patent dates and U.S. property stamp. Collection of SHM. NTP photo.

of the frame are the words, "from the sunken battleship Maine," and on the other side of the frame it reads, "July 1st 1898 /San Juan/ carried and used by Col. Theodore Roosevelt." Roosevelt's .38 can be seen at his home on Long Island at Sagamore Hill N.H.S.[13]

Lt. John C. Greenway of G-Troop, an ex-Yale man recruited by Roosevelt, has 2 revolvers attributed to him in the collections at AHS. The first piece is an 1877 Colt double action Lightning, serial #87035, 1892 manufacture. Greenway is wearing this revolver in the famous San Juan Hill photographs, standing just to Roosevelt's right. The second revolver is the standard Rough Rider issue side arm, a 5 1/2-inch barrel Colt single action in .45 long Colt, serial #7253.

The decision to side arm the Rough Riders with Colt single actions in .45 long Colt was a wise choice. Being Westerners and cowboys, most were very familiar with its use and shooting characteristics, maybe just a little too familiar, as they demonstrated one evening in Texas. During a patriotic band concert sponsored by the good citizens of San Antonio numerous Rough Riders shot up the place, causing quite a disturbance. The next day a local newspaper covered the story beginning with the headline, "Professor Beck's band played the cavalry charge and Rough Riders played hell."[14] Another breach of gun etiquette occurred when B Troop private William A. Owens shot out some lights on a street car and was afterwards referred to by his chums as "Smoke-'em-up-Bill."[15]

The Model 1873 Colt single action (single action refers to having to cock the hammer for each firing) .45 had seen hard frontier service over the last two decades prior to the war with Spain, and had earned a reputation as a dependable accurate and hard hitting side arm. First issued in a 7 1/2 inch barrel length then modified in the 1890s to a 5 1/2 inch barrel, officially known as "Colt's revolver, caliber .45, short barrel," by the Army.[16] Reducing the barrel length from 7 1/2 inches to 5 1/2 inches was done by both Colt and Springfield Armory. Originally modified (shortened) for use by Light Artillery Regiments, this revolver is universally known as the "Artillery Model Colt" by collectors today.

It is interesting to note that, as of this writing, the Colt Company still offers the model 1873 Single Action Army in their standard product line. Timeless testimony to the original design and "feel" of this weapon.

As with the Rough Rider carbines, issue numbers of Colt's revolvers for G & I Troops alone are known. The lowest serial number for this group is #1204 of 1874 manufacture, and the highest #189503, showing it was made a year after the fight in 1899. This is most likely a mistake from the hand-written records. 18xxx is the only number recorded in that range, and the serial number recorded just ahead of it is #139122. I believe #189503 should read #139503, with an 1891 manufacture, as the #8 and the #3 look similar, especially hand written.[17]

It should also be remembered that most "Artillery" Colts have mixed serial numbers on the components; i.e., numbers don't match.

The original service load for the .45 long Colt cartridge was 40 grains of black powder behind a round nose 255 grain lead bullet. This round produced a muzzle velocity of about 800 feet per second.[18]

The question of enlisted men keeping their sidearms after being dismounted in Florida and taking them to Cuba is unresolved. In fact, the author is unsure where the information originated that supports the idea the .45 Colts made it. Whether on the belt of a private or non-commissioned officer, a Colt pistol or the holster it is carried in can't be detected in any of the photographs taken after the dismount order in Tampa. Prior to that time these same side arms were an obvious object of pride and displayed openly for the photographer.

The decision to allow enlisted men to take their handguns or leave them would have been the commanding officer's call, if not from higher up. Given

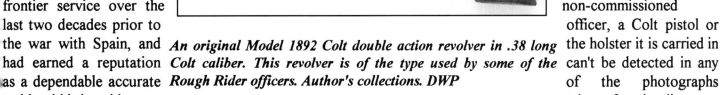

An original Model 1892 Colt double action revolver in .38 long Colt caliber. This revolver is of the type used by some of the Rough Rider officers. Author's collections. DWP

Original photo of Rough Riders loading their cartridge belts, quite possibly for the first time. The photograph was taken in Tampa, Florida. The soldier sitting at left has cavalry corporal stripes sewn to his trousers. The soldier sitting at right has cavalry sergeants stripes sewn to his trousers. Visible in the background are troop picket lines for the horses. The Man standing at left, looking over the Rough Rider's shoulder appears to be a civilian. Image courtesy PPLM.

Col. Wood's medical training and years of campaign experience, the added weight of the gun and ammunition in addition to the limited tactical value outweighed the supporting argument to bring them along. Regimental color and standard bearers, Troop guidon bearers, men attached to the Colt rapid fire, and dynamite gun crews might have sound reason to carry a sidearm as it would have been cumbersome to perform their tasks and lug a carbine as well. It should also be mentioned that the army made no provision for carrying a carbine on foot; i.e., no saddle scabbard or sling as the infantry had attached to their Krag rifles. To rule out all side arms for enlisted men going to Cuba is also illogical as some had special duties to perform.

In addition to a handgun, an officer could arm himself with a saber and a rifle. In 1898, the saber was more more a badge of rank than an effective weapon, especially dismounted. Roosevelt had this to say about his saber after the Las Guasimas fight, "I had left mine (his horse) at the beginning of the action, and was only regretting that I had not left my sword with it, as it kept getting between my legs when I was tearing my way through the jungle. I never wore it again in action."[19]

Only Wood and Roosevelt were horseback through much of the Cuban Campaign. The other Rough Rider officers were on foot the moment they landed on the beach. Doubtless they soon discovered the futility in carrying a saber long before Roosevelt did. Colonel Roosevelt's officer's quality saber is in the collections of Sagamore Hill N.H.S., Long Island, N.Y.

To what extent, or type of, long arms, or carbines were used by officers is unclear. Theodore Roosevelt mentioned that, "A few carried their favorite Winchesters using, of course, the New Model, which took the Government cartridge."[20] The New Model Winchesters, and government cartridge he refers to are the Model 1895 Winchester lever action and the .30 Krag round. How many of these "favorite" weapons were actually used in Cuba may never be known. There are no photographs or personal first hand accounts of

Original photograph of a Rough Rider hamming it up for the photographer. This photograph was taken at Camp Wikoff and appeared in Leslie's Weekly Magazine December 8, 1898. This is the only photo known to the author of a Rough Rider with a machete. The machete itself appears to be a Collins #22. The trooper is also carrying his Krag Jorgenson carbine suspended from his horse in the proper fashion. The trooper in the background is aiming his cocked revolver. Image courtesy OHS.

Rough Rider officers using this type of weapon at all in the Cuban campaign. The author believes these weapons never made it off the troop transport, *Yucatan*. Therefore, an officer had to rely on his primary weapon, that being the troops under his command.

A Model 1895 Winchester, serial number 7588 belonging to Roosevelt was used by Pvt. Robert D. Wrenn of A Troop, who joined the regiment in Tampa on June 4, much too late to be issued a precious Krag, so Roosevelt lent him his lever action. Theodore Roosevelt wrote, "(Bob Wrenn) had joined us very late and we could not get him a Krag carbine, so I had given him my Winchester, which carried the government (30-40) cartridge; and when he was mustered out he carried it home in triumph, to the envy of his fellows, who themselves had to surrender their beloved rifles."[21]

A mention should be made about machetes being issued to Rough Riders. Some believe machetes were given to enlisted men of 1st U.S. Volunteer Cavalry in lieu of regulation cavalry sabers. The intent, it seems, was to arm them with a better weapon with which to fight horseback as the Cuban rebels and Spanish troops did. The author believes the difference between a saber and machete used on horseback is slight at best. Theodore Roosevelt had this to say about arming the regiment with sabers "...it would be worse than a waste of time to try to train our men to use the saber--a weapon utterly alien to them...."[22]

The Regimental Adjutant Tom Hall had these remarks about the machetes given to the men, "None of the troops were supplied with machetes as had been originally intended. Later the detail assigned to the Colt rapid fire guns was armed with them..."[23] Negotiating heavy guns through dense underbrush alone justified their use.

Roger Fitch of G Troop made this related comment in his diary on August 7, ..."We had nothing to pack but our carbines, belts & canteens, besides our machetes etc." Note: to "pack" means to "carry."

Attached to the Rough Riders were three pieces of extra ordnance, two Colt rapid fire guns donated by wealthy New York citizens of 7.57 caliber capable of firing 500 rounds a minute. Ammunition was difficult to acquire for the Colt guns and at times captured Spanish rounds were used as it was in the caliber. Also under the command of the Rough Riders was an ordnance cannon called the Sims-Dudley dynamite gun that could lob a 4 1/2 inch charge of explosive gelatin equal in force to 9 lbs. of No. 1 dynamite.[24] Both Colt machine guns and the dynamite gun were heavy and slow to bring up the trail from the beach and thereby missed most of the fighting. After being entrenched at Fort Roosevelt on San Juan Hill, the Colt rapid fire guns and troublesome dynamite gun saw good service during the siege of Santiago while under the care of Lt. Parker of the 13th Infantry.

[1] *The Rough Riders,* by Theodore Roosevelt, page 9, New York, Scribners Sons, 1899.
[2] *The Krag Rifle,* by Lt. Col. William S. Brophy Page 3, The Gun Room Press, Highland Park N.J. 1995
[3] Ibid, page 5
[4] Ibid, page 6
[5] *The Krag Rifle Story,* Mallory & Olson Page 5, Springfield Research Service, 1980
[6] Ibid, page 5
[7] Ibid *The Krag Rifle* Page 49
[8] Ibid *The Krag Rifle Story* Page 144
[9] Ibid Page 146
[10] *Cartridges Of The World,* by Frank C. Barnes, Page 162, Digest Books, Inc. Northfield, Ill 1972
[11] Ibid, *Guns Of The Rough Riders,* Page 15
[12] *Theodore Roosevelt Outdoorsman,* By R.L. Wilson, Page 116. Winchester Press, N.Y. 1971
[13] Ibid, Page 115
[14] *The Arizona Rough Riders,* by Charles Herner Page 69, University Of Arizona Press, Tucson 1970
[15] Ibid Page 68
[16] *Guns Of The Rough Riders,* Part I, by Franklin B. Mallory, *Men At Arms,* NRA Journal, January/February 1989
[17] *Colts, Dates Of Manufacture* by R.L. Wilson, Pages 13 & 14, Simon & Schuster, N.Y. 1979
[18] *Cartridges Of The World,* Page 164
[19] Ibid, *The Rough Riders* Page 97
[20] Ibid, Pages 35,36
[21] Ibid Page 219
[22] Ibid Page 219
[23] *Fun And Fight Of The Rough Riders,* by Tom Hall, Page 62. Frederick A. Stokes Company, New York, 1899.
[24] *Roosevelts Rough Riders,* By Virgil Carrington Jones page 230, Doubleday & Company, N.Y.

Horse Equipment and the Mounted Pack

Original photograph of the 1st U.S. Volunteer Cavalry during mounted drill taken at Riverside Park, San Antonio, Texas. Eleven of the 12 troops are present in the photo. The troop not in the photos is probably still unequipped. An unidentified troop seen to the left of center row has many of its troopers without complete uniforms and some, in fact, in civilian clothing. Visible in the foreground are Col. Leonard Wood and on his left, Lt. Col. Theodore Roosevelt. Overall, the regiment displays a high degree of military bearing and preparedness. Certainly, a remarkable feat for such a short period of training. The high board fence surrounding Riverside Park is just visible in the far background. Image courtesy of SHM.

The heart and soul of a cavalry regiment are its horses, more so if 218 men of the regiment list their former occupation as being either cowboys, cattlemen or ranchers.[1] These volunteers would need the skills learned in their prior work after enlisting for service. Roosevelt noted "They were accustomed to handling wild and savage horses."[2] Horses were driven in small herds from the Depot at Fort Sam Houston, through the streets of San Antonio, to Camp Wood, the training grounds for the regiment. Each animal was to be of sound condition, weighing between 1,100-1,250 lbs, 15-15 1/2 hands high and broken to ride. What the Rough Riders got in reality was somewhat less. Judging from the photographs, many were light and some out and out small, weighing less than 800 lbs.

Troopers found that when they first sat upon their new mounts some bolted to a dead run, not heeding any signal to stop, others balked and reared up, dumping their riders or threw themselves on the ground, rider and all. A Troop private Arthur Tuttle recalled, "some of the damn horses bucked like hell."[3] All these irksome problems had to be dealt with, thus giving some an opportunity to show off their cowboy skills and perhaps to earn a little extra pocket money, schooling an unwilling bronc for a fellow trooper.

Colonel Wood gave the order to divide horses into troops by color. A Troop drew bays, B Troop - sorrels and C Troop received browns.[4] Information on the horse color of other troops is uncertain, yet the old black and white photos reveal that D and H troops had light colored horses called greys. With this added information a pattern emerges. If the rest of the regiment followed the same sequence pattern in horse color as that of the 1st Squadron, it would be as follows:

	Bays	Sorrels	Browns	Greys
1st Squadron	Troop A	Troop B	Troop C	Troop D
2nd Squadron	Troop E	Troop F	Troop G	Troop H
3rd Squadron	Troop I	Troop K	Troop L	Troop M

Note: light sorrels can be substituted for sorrels, blacks for bays and browns.

Cavalry commanders did this in an effort to recognize the different troops in the field if troop letters on the guidons could not be seen.

Officers could choose a mount out of the regiment's herd or purchase suitable horse flesh locally as Roosevelt did. "My own horses were purchased for me by a Texas friend, John Moore, with whom I had once hunted peccaries on the Nueces. I only paid fifty dollars a piece and the animals were not showy;.... but they were tough and hardy, and answered my purpose well."[5] Roosevelt took these two animals to Cuba, where the heavier of the two named Rain-in-the-face drowned with T.R.'s bedroll in the Daiquiri surf; the other, named "Texas," stayed through the entire campaign.

The saddles issued to the Rough Riders were of the McClellan pattern, first adopted for use by the U.S. Army in 1859. Since the 1859 model saddle many improvements or modifications were made to the original design. Leather was sewn over the wooden, rawhide covered tree to protect it from the elements. The stirrup size was enlarged to accommodate the rider's foot better; a horse hair cincha was added for the horse's comfort; and by 1896, an adjustable rigging system was ordered, but the design was still unmistakably of McClellan origin. In fact, the McClellan saddle stayed in service with the U.S. Army for nearly 100 years. The specific McClellan used by

Original photograph of B Troop, 1st U.S. Volunteer Cavalry, 1898. Not all members of B Troop are seen as only 39 are present in the picture. Capt. James Harvey McClintock is at the front of his troop. The company bugler is just to his left, rear. Another mounted officer pictured in the center of the photo is believed to be 1st Lt. George Wilcox. Also visible is the troop guidon carried in a specially equipped stirrup. Photo courtesy PPLM

the 1st U. S. Volunteer Cavalry is of the type referred to as the 1893 Godfrey Girth Modification.[6] The author was unable to locate an original model 1893 Godfrey saddle to examine. Information from saddle collectors and dealers in antique U.S. military equipment reveal that this type of saddle remains as one of the most difficult McClellan types to acquire in original condition and is very rare indeed.

The Capt. Godfrey (of the 7th Cavalry) improvement allowed the 2 1/2-inch rigging rings on the saddle some forward and backward movement. On previous saddle models no adjustment to the rigging could be made at all, a one-size-fits-all concept. The system permitted the saddle to alter itself to the horse's back somewhat, thus fitting a wider number of horse conformations. The 1893 Godfrey modification idea must have worked, resulting in fewer sore backs of the horses in use, and leading to the adoption of the Model 1896 saddle.[7] This adjustable rigging system was added to saddles already in use at the time that needed repair. The author has examined two Model 1885 saddles that have the Godfrey system on one side and the original 1885 rigging on the other. Only one side needed fixing. The alteration was also carried out on a number of saddles kept in storage.

Starting with a complete Model 1885 McClellan saddle, the Godfrey Modification was accomplished by first taking off the entire quarter strap assembly. The front and rear quarter straps and heart shaped safes were removed, leaving only a pair of 2 1/2 inch rings with the original tie straps attached. New, longer front and rear quarter straps were added, each end passing through the 2 1/2 inch ring and is attached behind the opposite strap, i.e. rear quarter strap was attached to the front quarter strap and the front was then attached to the rear.

A 5 1/2 x 6 1/2-inch shield shaped safe was added in back of the 2 1/2-inch ring by way of a 3/4-inch leather strap. This strap held the inner portions of the quarter strap assembly to the safe by way of three brass rivets, one on each end and one right in the center. All other aspects of the rigging remain the same and conform to the Model 1885 saddle specifications found in Ordnance Memoranda No. 29. Close examination by the author of three original Model 1885 saddle trees mainly show Model 1859 characteristics. At the end of the Civil War the government store houses had on hand a vast supply of saddle trees of 1859 pattern.[8] Our thrifty government decided to use these surplus trees in new model McClellans for the next thirty years.[9] It is safe to say that all the saddles issued to the Rough Riders could have been made on old Union army saddle trees.

The saddle itself was issued in three seat sizes, 11-inch, 11 1/2-inch and 12-inch. Using civilian measuring methods the same saddles would have the sizes of 14-inch, 14 1/2-inch and 15-inch seats.

A complete saddle is composed of one tree covered in 6-to 7-ounce leather, six coat straps permanently attached, two stirrup straps with hood stirrups and a complete quarter strap assembly with a horse hair cincha attached.

Other horse equipments issued to a Rough Rider seen in the original photographs are: one set of Model 1885 saddle bags with canvas liners, one model 1885 halter with lead strap; one complete Model 1874 curb bridle consisting of a curb bit with curb strap and reins, a link with snap hook used to connect riderless horses together and a 6-buckle headstall; one Model 1885 linen surcingle, one Model 1885 nose bag; one Model 1896 Krag carbine scabbard (all of the above items are made with black dyed leather); one Model 1885 saddle blanket, grey with yellow stripes.

Other horse items most likely issued to the 1st Volunteer Cavalry but not seen in the photographs are a curry comb, brush, watering bit, picket pin, lariat and a set of side lines.

---

[1] *Roosevelt's Rough Riders,* by Virgil Carrington Jones, page 342, Doubleday & Company, N.Y. 1971

[2] *The Rough Riders,* By Theodore Roosevelt, page 15 Scribners & Sons, N.Y. 1926

[3] *The Arizona Rough Riders,* by Charles Herner, page 63, University of Arizona Press, 1970

[4] Ibid pages 63 & 64

[5] Ibid *The Rough Riders,* page 34

[6] *The Evolution of the McClellan Cavalry Saddle,* by Dallas W. Freeborn, Military Collector and Historian, Summer 1979, page 60

[7] Ibid page 59

[8] Ibid page 61

[9] *Horse Equipments and Cavalry Accoutrements,* Ordnance Memoranda No. 29, by James S. Hutchins page 19, Westernlore Press, Tucson, Az 1984

Reproduction of Model 1885 saddle, altered to 1893 Godfrey specifications. Author's collection. Photograph DWP

Original photograph of Sgt. Arthur R. Perry, C Troop. Sgt. Perry has borrowed B Troops' Bill Owen's horse for the photograph as it most likely was quieter in nature. Plainly visible is the Model 1874 bridle with snaplink, Model 1885 saddle bags, and 1896 type 2 carbine scabbard attached. Please note Sergeant Perry's cowboy bandana. Image courtesy PPLM.

Troop H—Captain Curry—"Rough Riders."
Copyright 1898 by Strohmeyer & Wyman.

Original photograph of H Troop "standing-to-horse" taken at Tampa, Florida in 1898. Visible in the picture are the grey horses of H Troop. The saddle pack consisted of the following items attached to the saddle cantle: bed blanket, rolled inside the shelter tent. The 1885 nose bag is slipped over one end with its strap buckled around the other. Attached to the pommel are the trooper's rubber poncho and fatigue coat. The carbine in the foreground appears to have a breech cover attached, fabricated by the trooper. Trumpeter in foreground is wearing the proper government issue suspender. Also visible in the photograph are bandanas and a few cross saber insignias worn by the troopers. Image courtesy author's collection.

Tents, Blankets & Ponchos

Unidentified troopers at Tampa, Florida, photographed June 6, 1898. Soldiers seem busy preparing their equipment prior to leaving for Port Tampa. Visible in the photograph are soldiers rolling their bridles inside their horse blankets and buckling them to the cantle of the saddle. The saddle at left has attached I.D. card with trooper's name and company on it. It is interesting to note that these soldiers have yet to obtain cartridges, as none are seen in the belts. Image courtesy PPLM.

The recruits from the Arizona Territory arrived in San Antonio Friday morning the 6th of May 1898. Other men from New Mexico, Oklahoma, the Indian Territory, as well as recruits from the east showed up daily at the train depot and were taken to an improvised training grounds at Riverside Park. No tents were available for the enlisted men yet, so temporary shelter was provided under the roof of the exposition hall located on the park grounds. Eight wall tents for the officers were set up between the exposition hall and the park entrance.[1]

Shelter tents, along with other equipment were issued to the men all during the first and second weeks after their arrival at Riverside Park. The new uniforms and military routine must have given the volunteers a sense that they were now really in the army.

Moving out of the exposition hall, the men took up residence in their new shelter tents laid out in neat company streets with their company officer's tent nearby. Shelter tents were originally adopted during the Civil War in an effort to lighten the amount of baggage carried in wagons. Each man carried a tent half and, when fastened together with another, it became a suitable tent for two soldiers.

Early shelter tents were small and open at either end allowing the wind and rain to come in. Photographs of Rough Riders taken in San Antonio, Tampa and Cuba all reveal the use of the 1892 type shelter tent. The shelter tent adopted in 1892 appeared much the same as the older tents, but a triangular piece of material was added to one end, allowing the tent to be closed. This not only helped keep the weather out, but effectively lengthened the tent.[2] Specifications for the Model 1892 tent are: to be made of 8-ounce cotton duck, with dimensions of 61 inches high and 65 inches along the ridge, with a 47 x 43-inch triangular piece at one end.

D Troop, Camp Tampa, probably June 6, 1898. Having received orders to dismount and act as infantry, the Rough Riders have transferred their blankets, ponchos and shelter tents into a horseshoe-shaped roll that rests on their left shoulders. These soldiers appear to have lost some of their military neatness, as time would not allow instruction as to proper wearing of equipment dismounted. Please note second man in file has fabricated breach cover. Image courtesy PPLM.

There were nine metal buttons along the top and seven along the back piece. It was also referred to as a "double tent." The Model 1892 tent specifications were reprinted in May 1894 and again in June 1896.[3] Issued with each shelter half are to be one 6-foot by 1/4-inch manila rope, four wooden stakes, and one two-piece wooden pole, one piece of the pole having a 4-inch tin socket attached to hold the two pieces together.

The author has seen original examples of this tent with branch unit, company and personal number markings stenciled in black on the surface of the canvas.

It was common practice for troops to pile their bedrolls and haversacks just before being deployed for action. If left unguarded by a soldier from the same unit, the risk of thievery was high.

Cuban irregulars (untrained soldiers) usually got the blame for this outrage and were not well thought of by the Rough Riders. Perhaps the Cubans justified their poor conduct toward their American allies because of the greater need on their part. Most all in the rebel Cuban army were starved scarecrows in rags, some having no uniforms or clothing at all. As previously mentioned, many Rough Riders had their equipment piles ransacked. While fighting on June 24 at Las Guasimas the Rough Riders had much of their blankets, tents, food and other supplies stolen. Many had to improvise to get by, making crude shelters from palm fronds and remaining tent halves. Some just stayed in the open.

By the first week in August, the regiment was preparing to leave the trenches. Pvt. Fitch related: "August 7. busy in A.M., getting ready to move...we left our shelter tent standing & our rolls (blankets and ponchos) were carried to the boat on wagons."[4] Being instructed to leave their old shelter tents in Cuba, the Rough Riders boarded transport and made way for the detention camp at Wikoff, Long Island. Waiting for them were new larger tents already pitched and laid out in company streets. Called Improved Common Tents by the Quartermaster, the 6-foot-11 x 8-foot-4 base and ample 6-foot-10-inch height roof surely must have seemed an improvement.[5]

As was the practice at that time, discharged servicemen were allowed by the army to retain their blankets and take them home. The Rough Rider Museum in Las Vegas, New Mexico possesses two Model 1876 bed blankets with 1st U.S. Volunteer Cavalry attribution. The Army Quartermaster in January 1885 gives these specifications for the above blanket size to be 84 inches long and 66 inches wide. Color was to be blue and white mixed (making a bluish grey), with a 2 1/2-inch to 3-inch wide dark blue stripe across the top and bottom about 6 inches from the edge. Each blanket to have the letters "U.S." 4 inches long in the center and to conform in color to the stripes, and maybe either woven into the fabric or stamped on the blanket. To weigh not less than five pounds.[6] Like the tents and haversacks, many of these blankets were "lost" to the "depraved" Cubans.

A rubber poncho was issued to each enlisted man in the Rough Riders. Originally given to soldiers in the mounted service during the Civil War, they were, in actual practice, used by dismounted troops as well. Rubber ponchos were made of cotton sheeting coated with rubber, 45 inches by 72 inches. A 14-inch slit or opening in the center of the poncho allowed the soldier's head to poke through so it could be worn as a cape. The slit was closed with a pressed-on button and hole, permitting the poncho also to be used as a blanket or shelter. The outer edge is fitted with sixteen 1/4-inch brass grommets, reinforced with a 1 1/2-inch square of same material as the poncho.[7]

An attributed rubber poncho used by Rough Rider J.B. Brady is in the collection of the Sharlot Hall Museum, Prescott, Arizona.

Once away from the well supplied camps at San Antonio and Tampa the officers of the regiment on campaign ared much the same as the enlisted men, being reduced to what they

Pvt. Louis Gasser, H Troop, September, 19, 1898 at Camp Wikoff. Here he is seen still wearing his brown fatigues. Records indicate Louis Gasser received a late promotion before being mustered out of service. Of interest are the common tents placed in company streets in the background. Though his trousers and leggings are heavily worn and stained, this proud soldier has chosen to retain them. Image courtesy HHLRC.

Original photograph of a company street taken in early June, 1898, Tampa, Florida. E Troop guidon is just visible at right. The troopers have arranged their horse equipment neatly in front of their Model 1892 tents. Of interest are the sticks used as tent poles, as the regulation two-piece poles were not issued. Image courtesy PPLM.

could carry in a bed roll over their shoulders. Officers shared the same hardships as their men under their command. A few officers brought their own equipment from home.

In this telegram from Roosevelt to his friend Robert Ferguson, he advised him on what to bring to Texas. Printed here through the courtesy of AHS, Tucson

April 29, 1898

My Dear Bob,

I have received your letter of yesterday. All your equipment, arms, and horses will be furnished. You will of course be ready. I will telegraph you when I want you to go. A lot of Harvard fellows are going as troopers. I should take down a rubber blanket and your own plaid. In great haste.

                                        T. Roosevelt

The "plaid" Roosevelt mentions might also refer to a "mackintosh" he speaks of just after the Daiquiri landing.[8] The author thinks they are both a type of light wool blanket woven in a tartan design.

The officers personal shelter and comfort improved greatly at Camp Wikoff, Long Island. Roosevelt stayed in two back to back 14-foot 6-inch x 14-foot hospital wall tents.[9] The front tent served as an office with the one behind as his personal quarters.

[1] *Roosevelt's Rough Riders*, by Virgil Carrington Jones page 31,32, Doubleday & Company, N.Y. 1971.

[2] *Shelter Tents Used in 1898*, by Steve Gay and Dave Jones paper prepared by Spanish American War Students, no publisher or date.

[3] The Journal #17, Article entitled U.S. "Army Tents of The Spanish War," by Mike Lewis 1997.

[4] Roger Fitch, G Troop, personal diary, Rough Rider Museum, Las Vegas, N.M.

[5] *U.S. Army Uniforms and Equipment*, 1889 by Quartermaster General of the Army, page 219, Forward by Jerome A. Golden, University of Nebraska Press..

[6] Ibid page 26.

[7] Ibid page 240.

[8] *The Rough Riders,* by Theodore Roosevelt page 75 Scribners Sons, N.Y. 1899.

[9] Ibid *U.S. Army Uniforms and Equipment*. Pgs. 202-204.

Regimental Flags

Cavalry regiments of this period were authorized to carry in the field one national standard, one cavalry standard, and one guidon for every troop.

The national standard of stars and stripes flown by the Rough Riders was not a regulation flag, but a handmade gift from the Women's Relief Corps of Phoenix, Arizona. The flag was presented to the Arizona contingent by Governor McCord at a ceremony held in Prescott, May 4, 1898. The flag itself measures 91 inches on the fly and 50 inch on the pole. The blue field is 26 1/4 inches high ending on the 4th red stripe down, and measures 34 inches from the pole binding. The end of the flag is finished in a 3 1/2-inch fold and is stitched back on the body, a 1 1/4-inch wide binding is sewn to the body at the other end and four 1/2-inch brass grommets are attached, one at top and bottom, and two evenly spaced between. The white stars are sewn in a random pattern on the blue field. The flag is fastened by four leather thongs to a 96 inch long 1 1/2-inch diameter wooden pole. The spear point is made of copper metal filled with concrete and is approximately 10-inch long, making the total length of the pole 106 inches. 1 1/4-inch wide red, white, and blue ribbons are wound around the pole beginning at the top and ending just below the flag and are tied off.

The New Mexican Volunteers likewise received a national flag from the patriotic citizens of their territory. Funds to purchase the flag were raised through private donations, the wife of Territorial Governor Otero making the first contribution of $10.00 toward the effort. The New Mexico flag measures 61 inches on the pole and 70 1/2 inches on the fly, and is trimmed in gold. The pole is topped with a braided eagle with hanging golden tassels, truly an emblem to make any regiment proud. The above flag is currently in the collections of the Palace of the Governors, Santa Fe, N.M. After the presentation of the flag, Maj. Hersey was selected to take the flag and deliver it to the regiment at San Antonio, obviously intending that it be the national standard of the Rough Riders. This was not to be as the Arizona Squadron were first in Texas, and they were not about to give up the coveted honor of using the flag they brought with them. The author found no evidence of the New Mexico flag being taken to Cuba. It is doubtful that more than one national flag was carried during the Cuban Campaign, as the regimental commander is usually in very close proximity to the colors, and having more than one would be confusing to those seeking him.

Original Rough Rider stars and stripes as presented by Governor McCord to the Arizona Squadron. The flag has been removed from its pole. It rests here in a display case at the state capitol museum in Phoenix, Arizona. Photo courtesy Michael Carmen.

Another type of flag carried by the Rough Riders was the Cavalry Standard. Regulations describe the flag as follows: "The regimental standard will be of yellow silk, 4 feet on the fly and 3 feet on the lance, which will be 9 feet 6 inches long, including spear and ferrule. The coat of arms of the United States embroidered in silk on the center, beneath the eagle a red scroll, with number and name of regiment embroidered in yellow, fringe yellow."[1] The soldier assigned to carry the cavalry standard was Sgt. Nevin P.

Sgt. Albert P. Wright of C Troop standing with Rough Rider colors at Camp Wikoff, Long Island. Being the tallest man in the regiment, at 6-foot-6, Wright had the honor of carrying the colors all through the Cuban campaign. This tattered but proud emblem of the regiment received three separate holes made by Spanish mausers. In the background the cavalry standard and another Stars and stripes is clearly visible. Image courtesy HHLRC

Gutilius of H Troop, a 44-year-old miner from Tularosa, New Mexico.[2] Roosevelt mentioned him later saying, "Sergeant Guitilias, a gallant old fellow, a veteran of the Civil War, whose duties were properly those of standard-bearer, he having charge of the yellow cavalry standard of the regiment; but in the Cuban campaign he was given more active work of helping run the dynamite gun."[3] The original cavalry standard of the Rough Riders now hangs in display a Sagamore Hill National Historic Sight, Long Island.

Each of the 12 troops in the regiment carrie guidons marked with the letter of the troop or compan and regimental number. The guidons for troops G an B of the Rough Riders have been examined by th author. Both are made of wool bunting, and adhere t the regulations described in 1895, which are "cu

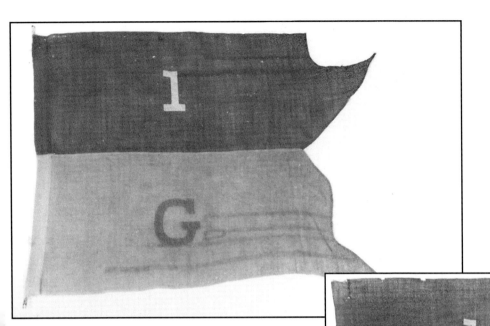

Above: Original guidon carried by G Troop, Rough Rider showing repair made to the swallow-tail. Collection of AHS.

Right: Guidon carried by B Troop, Rough Riders. Collections SHM.

Below: Original guidon lance carried by G Troop, detailing spear and ferrule. Collections AHS. All photos DWP.

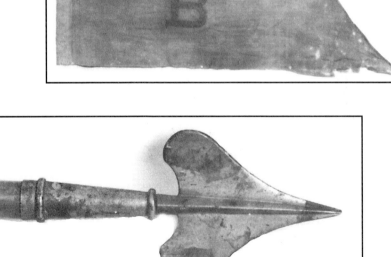

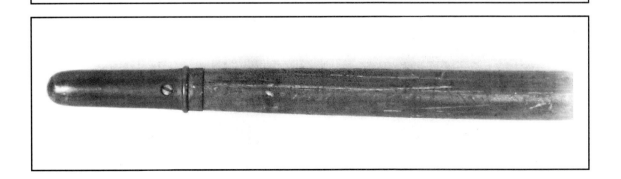

Original photo of H Troop mounted, Tampa, Florida, 1898. Plainly visible at left is the company guidon bearer. Note especially equipped stirrup with socket attached. Image courtesy PPLM.

COWBOYS IN UNIFORM

Original photo of rough Riders at Camp Wikoff awaiting the arrival of President McKinley. The guidons of E, G and I Troops are plainly visible. Image courtesy HHLRC.

swallow-tailed, 15 inches to the fork, 3 feet 5 inches fly from the lance to the end of the swallow tail, and 2 feet 3 inches on the lance, having two horizontal stripes each one-half the width of the flag, the upper red and the lower white, the red stripe having on both sides in the center the number of the regiment in white, (No. 1 for the Rough Riders) and the white stripe the letter of the troop in red (either A,B,C,D,E,F,G,H,I,K,L, or M, there is no J Troop) the letter and number block - shaped, 4 3/4 inches high the lance 1 1/4-inch diameter and 9 feet long, including spear and ferrule.[4] Even though dismounted it appears the regiment took their troop guidons with them to Cuba. An original picture of Rough Riders hitching a ride to Port Tampa in coal cars clearly shows the guidon for K Troop being taken along. Admittedly, maybe it was not a good idea to have the guidons when acting as infantry attempting to conceal their location from the enemy. Perhaps they were brought along because of the need to help keep the men with their respective troops, or maybe guidons were just good for the morale of the horse soldiers, so recently dismounted.

[1] *Regulations for the United States Army, 1895*, Sections 215 & 218, Government Printing Office 1895, Washington, D.C.
[2] *Roosevelt's Rough Riders*, by Virgil Carrington Jones, page 301, Doubleday & Company, N.Y. 1971
[3] *The Rough Riders*, by Theodore Roosevelt, page 164. Scribners Sons, New York, 1899
[4] IBID, *Regulations for the U.S. Army 1895*, Section 221.

Souvenirs and Mementos

Soldiers through the ages have always brought home souvenirs to remind themselves and their loved ones of war time experiences. Though that object may seem trivial to some, to the old soldier, the object is a priceless keepsake, that when looked upon brings back a flood of memories.

Fortunately, the officers and enlisted men of the Rough Riders were no different. One noteworthy officer of the regiment excelled at this custom of sending home souvenirs, Lt. John C. Greenway of Hot Springs, Arkansas. The inventory list of items sent home by this officer is impressive. It includes a Krag carbine, a short barrel Colt .45, a Colt lightning (his personal side-arm used through the war), an American bugle. His captured plunder includes a Spanish Mauser rifle and bayonet, two machetes, the list goes on from there. Because of Greenway's efforts and others like him, the student of history has material to examine.

Some in the Rough Riders were content to simply bring home their old grey bed blankets or maybe just a piece of army bread call hard tack, as Private Misner of B troop did. As it turns out, this single piece of Spanish American War hard tack remains as one of the few in existence, and therefore is a valuable artifact. These little items offer rare insight into the daily life of the soldier.

Some mementos take on a high degree of importance. Perhaps it once belonged to a cherished friend or comrade, struck down in his prime. The people of Arizona still hold Capt. William (Buckey) O'Neil's memory dear, and to see his pocket watch he was wearing when killed brings us closer to our hero.

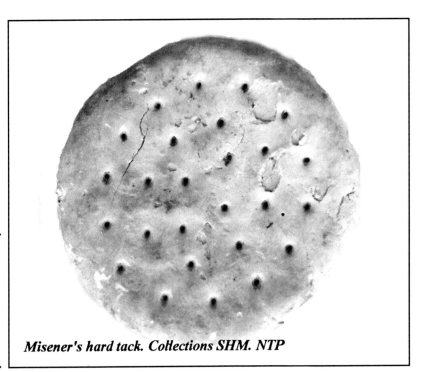
Misener's hard tack. Collections SHM. NTP

After the war, Theodore Roosevelt became one of the most admired and influential Presidents the United States has ever had. Though he was the elected leader of the new world power, he never forgot his Rough Riders, attending the many reunions when ever he could. A veteran organization presented him with a special medal for his service with the Rough Riders during the war. Mr. Roosevelt carried this same medal as a watch fob daily, all through his presidency and much of his civilian life until his death. The ties between Roosevelt and the men that served under him were close indeed and his medal reminded him always as he checked the time of day.

Pvt. Fitch of G Troop recorded in his diary on July 1, the day of the assault on San Juan, "I picked up a bullet and pulled out a bayonet from a Spanish gun as mementos, the last being very useful in pounding coffee (beans), splitting wood, etc.[1] Captured enemy cartridges seem to have been a favorite souvenir of the Rough Riders. Most collections the author observed dealing with Rough Rider Artifacts had Spanish ammunition included. Col. Roosevelt himself commented in a letter to his sister, a day after the Las Guasimas fight,"...I kept three of the empty cartridges we got from a dead Spaniard at this point, for the children."[2] The Spanish mauser fired a 7x57 cartridge, the same as used in the Colt rapid fire guns attached to the regiment. Live ammunition of this size found on the battlefield was often pressed into use and fed through the Colt guns.

Another Spanish cartridge, the .43 caliber was also much sought after by Rough Riders as trophies. Called

Bucky O'Neil's Watch

Capt. William O'Neil's railroad pocket watch he was wearing at the time of his death, July 1, 1898. Collections SHM. NTP.

Left: The medal used as a watch fob by Roosevelt during his presidency.

polka-dot, "neck rags," as cowboys call them, became the signature trademark of the regiment. A very few have survived.

[1] Rodger Fitch, G-troop, personal diary, Rough Rider Museum, Las Vegas, N.M.
[2] *Theodore Roosevelt Outdoorsman,* by R.L. Wilson, Page 116, Winchester Press, N.Y. 1971.

On the Back Cover:

Upper left: Model 1894 leggings worn by Pvt. Charles O. Hopping of F troop of Santa Fe, New Mexico. Worn in Cuba.

Upper right: Medals awarded to Pvt. Frank C. Brito, H Troop of El Paso, Texas.

Bottom left: Canteen carried by Hopping, A Troop's Oscar Wager's cup showing the effects of a Spanish bullet. Crucifix, coffee and sugar bags of Robert Denny of I Troop who did not go to Cuba.

Bottom right: Battlefield souvenirs brought home by Rough Riders. Spent Hotchkiss brass, Spanish hat cucade, Spanish ammo pouch, a card with Spanish uniform buttons affixed, a 30/40 Krag and 7.57 Spanish ammunition.

the "Poison Bullet" by many soldiers, the projectile in fact was only brass plated, and when carried in leather boxes as the Spanish did, soon became covered with verdigris. Some U.S. troops were convinced the bullets were coated in a fowl poison.

While the regiment was waiting at Camp Tampa for the invasion to begin, Roosevelt, as well as some of the men, purchased cotton bandanas. It's reported that two young Jewish lads invested $300 of their capital into blue and red polka-dot bandanas. They wandered the camps of the different regiments selling to any and all. The Rough Riders were good customers. These

Summary

I must confess, in 1979 my image of the Rough Riders was that of a loose run, come-as-you-are outfit exuding an almost "Wild West show" atmosphere wherever they went. As the research progressed and the more I learned, the less the previous assessment held true. I found them instead to have strong leadership, be properly equipped, and to a man, focused on the job at hand. I believe, given another five or six weeks training, the 1st U.S. Volunteer Cavalry would have become a showcase of military bearing on a level which could be compared with any regular cavalry regiment of the time.

We must realize that four weeks' training is all any Rough Rider recruit received, many getting much less, some joining up just as the unit was ready to sail to Cuba. Photographic evidence also reveals that it is unlikely a Rough Rider live-fired his carbine in practice.

The only time Rough Riders can be seen with cartridges in their belts is just prior to boarding transport for Cuba. In today's military it would be unthinkable to send new troops into combat without extensive training using live ammunition. Perhaps .30-.40 ammunition was too scarce and couldn't be wasted on practice fire. Or possibly the men from the west were considered skilled enough with any weapon for the task ahead.

We also know that most of the Colt revolvers were left behind in Florida with the rest of the regiment. I am positive that if they had taken their pistols with them to Cuba, the stories of its effective use during close fighting on San Juan and Kettle Hills would have been proven.

Proof of officers actually using Model 1895 Winchesters in combat is so far nonexistent. We do have good records of one being used by Bob Wrenn, an enlisted man.

With the exception of their fatigue uniform and lack of issue sabers, the Rough Riders were equipped much the same as any cavalry regiment in the regular army. Saddles, tents, canteens, mess tins, rubber ponchos, weapons, everything given to the Rough Riders was the same as issued to the regulars. The Krag carbine was by far the single most valuable piece of equipment the regiment was issued. It allowed them to fight alongside the regulars and on an even footing against the Spanish. Without the Krag, it is doubtful the story of the 1st U.S. Volunteers would have been as brilliant.

In order for the new volunteers to be taken seriously, they had to look and act the part. Invasion planners of the general staff were not about to include a unit that did not look prepared with a brigade of regulars that did.

Much was accomplished during their short training time in San Antonio. The lion's share of the credit for this must go to the efforts and effectiveness of Rough Rider officers. Wood and Roosevelt had the political connections to see the regiment got the proper equipment in time. Colonel Wood was the military man with hard campaign experience. Lt. Colonel Roosevelt, though a civilian, knew how to handle the proud Westerners and was a natural leader. Squadron and troop officers were chosen to command on the requirements of military experience or were men already known for their bravery and leadership qualities.

The willing attitude of the average enlisted man to learn from these officers also played a key role in the success of the regiment. Each trooper knew that the freedom of the oppressed Cuban people and the reputation of their home territories depended on their actions.

The standard uniform for Rough Rider officers and enlisted men alike were altered Model 1884 fatigues. Enlisted rank insignia and yellow facing cloth for officers were sewn directly onto the brown fatigues, a practice that was forbidden in the regular army. Most of these brown canvas fatigue uniforms were destroyed in Cuba. Only McClintock and Palmer's exist today. A second issue in Cuba of Model 1898 Khaki uniforms were to replace those uniforms worn-out in service. Some uniforms were privately purchased on the soldiers' own initiative. During their interment at Camp Wikoff all uniforms types were worn, along with some civilian dress. It is my sincere hope that because of this book, more items with Rough Rider usage might be identified.

Jack Stewart
1998

Excerpts from the Cavalry Drill Regulation, 1896

United States Army

27. This school has for its object the instruction of the individual recruit, on foot, and afterward that of the squad.

From the beginning, the instructor will insist upon smart appearance of the recruits, and will exact that their clothing be clean and neatly adjusted.

33. To teach the recruits how to assemble, the instructor will first place them in a single rank arranged according to height, the tallest man on the right with intervals of two inches, as nearly as may be between men, and explain that the object of the interval are to give freedom of movement in marching and in the use of the carbine in rank: then direct them to open out the right elbow slightly until the left elbow of the man on the right is lightly touched and then withdraw the elbow; this repeated a few times, he will cause the recruits to fall out and placing the man on the right in position will instruct them that at the command *fall in* they will successively and quickly take their places in ranks as before, each assuring himself of the interval by making touch by the elbow and then withdrawing the elbow. He then commands: *Fall in*. Each recruit takes his place as he judges correct and then opens out slightly his right elbow, and moves, if necessary, a little to the right or left until his right elbow touches lightly the left elbow of the man next to the right and then closes his elbow to the habitual position. The instructor verifies the intervals.

Position of the Soldier, or Attention.

35. Heels on the same line, and as near each other as the conformation of the man permits.

Feet turned out equally, and forming with each other an angle of about 60 degrees.

Knees straight without stiffness.

Body erect on the hips, inclining a little forward; shoulders square and falling equally.

Arms and hands hanging naturally, backs of the hands outward; little fingers opposite the seams of the trousers; elbows near the body.

Head erect and square to the front; chin slightly drawn in, without constraint; eyes straight to the front.

36. Being at the halt, to rest the men: FALL OUT, or rest, or at east.

At the command fall out, the men may leave the ranks but will remain in the immediate vicinity.

At the command fall in, they resume their former places at attention.

The the command rest, the men keep one heel in place but are not required to preserve silence or immobility.

If marching: 1. Route order, 2. March: or, 1. At ease, 2. March.

The men keep either places in the squad but are not required to keep the cadenced step: at route order, they are not required to preserve silence.

To resume the attention: Attention.

The men take the position of the soldier and fix their attention.

37. 1 Parade, 2. Rest.

Carry the right foot six inches straight to the rear, left knee slightly bent: clasp the hands in front of the center of the body, left hand uppermost, left thumb clasped by thumb and forefinger of right hand: preserve silence and steadiness of position.

38. To resume the attention or position of the soldier: Attention.

The men take the position of the soldier and fix their attention.

39. To dismiss the squad: Dismissed.

Salute with the Hand.

43. 1. *Right (or Left) hand*, 2. Salute.

Raise the right hand smartly till the forefinger touches the lower part of the head-dress above the right eye, thumb and fingers extended and joined, palm to the left forearm inclined at about 45 degrees, hand and wrist straight; at the same time look toward the person to be saluted. (Two) Drop the arm quietly by the side.

If uncovered, the forefinger touches the forehead above the eye.

The salute for officers is the same; the left hand is used only when the right is engaged.

Position of Order Arms.

70. The butt rests evenly on the ground arms hanging naturally, elbows near the body, right hand holding the piece between the thumb and fingers, first two fingers in front, the others in rear; the toe of the piece on a line with and touching the toe of the right shoe.

On first bearing arms, the recruits are liable to derange their positions by lowering a shoulder or hip. The instructor endeavors to correct these faults.

71. *Being at the order:* 1. Present, 2. ARMS.

Raise and carry the piece with the right hand in front of the center of the body, barrel to the rear and vertical, at the same time grasp it with the left hand at the balance, forearm horizontal and resting against the body. (Two) Grasp the small of the sock with the right hand below the guard.

72. *Being at the present:* 1. Order, 2. ARMS.

Let go with the right hand and regrasp the piece above the rear sight: let go with the left hand and lower the piece with the right. (Two) Lower the piece gently to the ground with the right hand, drop the left by the side, and take the position or order arms.

73. Being at the order: 1. Port, 2. Arms.

Raise and throw the piece diagonally across the body with the right hand, magazine to the front, grasp it smartly at the small of the stock: the left, palm up, at the balance, thumb clasping the piece, barrel sloping to the left and crossing opposite the junction of the neck with the left shoulder: right forearm horizontal; left forearm resting against the body; right forearm and piece near the body.

74. *Being at the order:* 1. *Right shoulder*: 2. ARMS.

Raise and throw the piece diagonally across the body, as in port arms, except that the right hand embraces the butt, heel between the first and second fingers. (TWO) Raise the piece and place it on the right shoulder, barrel up, and muzzle elevated so as not to interfere with the men in rear, trigger guard in front of, and near the right shoulder; the piece so held that when viewed from the front, it will appear nearly parallel to the row of buttons, right elbow down; slip the left hand down to the handle. (THREE) Drop the left hand by the side.

75. *Being at the right shoulder:* 1. *Order*, 2. ARMS. Lower the butt quickly and to the right, and take the first position of right shoulder from order. (TWO) Lower the piece with the left hand, at the same time regrasping it with the right above the sight and take the first position of order from present. (THREE) Take the position of order arms.

76. *Being at the right shoulder*: 1. *Port*, 2. ARMS.

Take the first position of right shoulder from order. (TWO) Take the position of port arms.

1. Right shoulder, 2. ARMS. Take the first position of right shoulder from the order. (TWO) Take the second position of right shoulder from the order. (THREE) Drop the left hand by the side.

78. *Being at the order:* 1. *Parade*, 2. *Rest*.

Carry the right foot six inches straight to the rear, left knee slightly bent: carry the muzzle in front of the center of the body, barrel to the left, right hand near the muzzle, and take the position of parade rest (par. 37) muzzle between thumb and forefinger of the left hand.

Attention. Quit the piece with the left hand, and resume the order.

Inspection of Carbines

121. *Being at the order*: 1. *Inspection*, 2. CARBINE.

Execute port arms; open the magazine gate; open the chamber and place the right hand on the butt, the heel between the first and second fingers.

The inspector takes the piece (the man dropping the hands by the side), inspects, and hands it back to the man; the man receives it with the left hand at the balance, closes chamber, closes the magazine gate, pulls the trigger, and takes the position of order arms.

Original photograph of E Troop's company street taken at Camp Wikoff. The soon to be discharged soldiers are packing and inventorying their equipment. Image courtesy HHLRC.